MARCO POLO

FRENCH ATLANTIC COAST

GREAT BRITAIN

Paris

Seine

Loire

Nantes

FRANCE

Dijon

French Atlantic Coast

Lyon

Bordeaux

Rhône

SPAIN

AND.

SYMBOLS

INSIDER TIP	Insider Tip
★	Highlight
●●●●	Best of ...
☆	Scenic view
☺	Responsible travel: fair trade principles and the environment respected
(*)	Telephone numbers that are not toll-free

PRICE CATEGORIES HOTELS

Expensive   over 100 euros

Moderate   70–100 euros

Budget   under 70 euros

Price for 2 people in a double room without breakfast in the high season

PRICE CATEGORIES RESTAURANTS

Expensive   over 40 euros

Moderate   25–40 euros

Budget   under 25 euros

Price of an average 3-course meal. Set meals include a cheap table wine. Eating à la carte is much more expensive

On the cover: the Île de Ré off La Rochelle p. 50 | Fleur de sel de Guérande p. 36

CONTENTS

Côte d'Argent → p. 64

Côte Basque → p. 84

Trips & Tours → p. 96

Road atlas → p. 126

MAPS IN THE GUIDEBOOK

(128 A1) Page numbers and coordinates refer to the road atlas

Coordinates are also given for places that are not marked on the road atlas

Street maps of Biarritz, Bordeaux, La Rochelle and Nantes can be found inside the back cover

**INSIDE BACK COVER:
PULL-OUT MAP →**

PULL-OUT MAP

(∅ A–B 2–3) Refers to the removable pull-out map

The best MARCO POLO Insider Tips

Our top 15 Insider Tips

INSIDER TIP Wafer-thin delicacies

You won't be able to resist the crêpes and *galettes* at La Fraiseraie in Nantes served with a range of exotic fillings such as *foie gras* or scallops → **p. 41**

INSIDER TIP Home-baked culture

The former LU biscuit factory in Nantes is now a popular venue for cultural events (photo right) → **p. 42**

INSIDER TIP Cabanes art

Strict EU hygiene regulations have led to something very positive. 18 former oyster farmers' huts in the fishing port at Château-d'Oléron have now been turned into arts and crafts workshops → **p. 48**

INSIDER TIP Salt ice cream

The ice cream parlour La Martinière in Saint-Martin-de-Ré, the main town on the island, has a number of exotic flavours on offer – such as the mildly salty variety made with *fleur de sel* from the island's own salt pans → **p. 53**

INSIDER TIP Paradise with breakfast

Staying in the small hotel Blanc Marine on Noirmoutier is like visiting old friends. The hearty breakfast served by your hosts is wonderful in its own right → **p. 59**

INSIDER TIP Wine directly from the producer

Dozens of wines made by the lady of the house herself line the shelves in the winebar La Robe in Bordeaux for all to enjoy → **p. 73**

INSIDER TIP Just say cheese

Cheese lovers make a beeline for Baud & Millet in Bordeaux where the restaurant serves a phenomenal 200 different types of cheese – which you can also stock up on for home → **p. 73**

INSIDER TIP River bed

If you're fond of unconventional places to stay, try 'Le D'Ô'. This one-roomed hotel is a boat moored on the Erdre, a tributary close to the heart of Nantes → **p. 43**

INSIDER TIP Stand-up paddling: surfers eat your heart out

Anyone who paddles across Arcachon Bay standing up sees things in a very different light. Give this trend-setting sport a try – it's easier than it looks! Paddle to the oyster beds or the Dune du Pilat → **p. 67**

INSIDER TIP Feel like the king of the castle

Château Franc Mayne in Saint-Émilion is beautifully furnished and guests can sample the château's own wines – this is after all Bordelais (photo left) → **p. 77**

INSIDER TIP Snail ravioli and coconut ice cream

The Restaurant Le Square in Nantes comes up with innovative interpretations of classical French dishes at affordable prices. Why not sample snail ravioli with cream of cress, lobster with ginger and coriander and a hint of Asia, or passion fruit with coconut ice cream – pure bliss! → **p. 42**

INSIDER TIP Fit for a king

Maison Adam in Saint-Jean-de-Luz, founded in 1660, produces delicious almond macaroons that are reputed to have been served at Louis XIV's wedding and are still made to the same recipe → **p. 94**

INSIDER TIP Live like Eleanor of Aquitaine

The four hotel rooms in Les Jardins d'Aliénor on Oléron have been individually furnished with loving care → **p. 48**

INSIDER TIP Luxury treats

De luxe ice cream and sorbets are made by hand at Jerôme's in Biarritz and served in a post-modernist setting → **p. 88**

INSIDER TIP Take a walk around the ponds

Stroll through the middle of the famous oyster beds of Marennes-Oléron at Bourcefranc-le-Chapus which have changed little over the years → **p. 104**

BEST OF ...

FOR FREE

● *Booty on the beach*

So you still need something for dinner tonight? The tide can give you a helping hand – for free. At low tide, the sea leaves some of its treats on the sand for people to gather quite legitimately. In the meantime, *pêche-à-pied* has become quite a popular pastime along the Atlantic coast → **p. 21**

● *A view open to all*

It may not be the Eiffel Tower but Gustave worked on this building too. In Arcachon you can climb to the top of the *Observatoire Sainte-Cécile* from where you have a free view over the rooftops of the town and its lovely villas that is green in winter too → **p. 66**

● *Boating on the Loire*

Boat trips don't have to be expensive. Along the lower reaches of the Loire between Le Pellerin and Couëron and between Indret and Basse-Indre you can take the *ferry* across the river – for nothing! → **p. 41**

● *Lovely views of the castle in Nantes*

A wonderful view of the Château des ducs de Bretagne can be had for free if you take the 500m *round walk* along the fortified ramparts. Even if you don't visit the exhibitions inside, you can still get a good idea of the castle's architecture from here → **p. 38**

● *Visit a wine producer*

Red wine from the Médoc peninsula is world famous. Almost all producers have *wine tasting* arrangements when you can sample the different vintages. Wine tasting is not only informative – it is usually free too, such as in Pauillac (photo) → **p. 81**

● *Museums for free*

Admission to some museums is free on certain days. Careful planning certainly pays off, especially for families. Everything you always wanted to know about Basque culture, for example, can be found free of charge on the first Sunday in the month in the excellent *Musée Basque* in Bayonne → **p. 90**

●●●● Dots in guidebook refer to 'Best of ...' tips

ONLY ON THE ATLANTIC COAST
Unique experiences

● *Oysters from the farmer*

They don't come fresher than this! Enjoy oysters in the most traditional way possible in a *cabane*, one of the little oyster farmers' huts that have been converted into restaurants such as *Le Relais des Salines* on Oléron. *Huîtres* instead of chips and ketchup is the catchword in such 'snack bars'! → p. 49

● *A stroll around the salt pans*

Coarse sea salt and exquisite *fleur de sel* are must-haves among all the souvenirs to take back after a visit to the west coast of France. The *Musée des Traditions de l'Île* on Noirmoutier shows how the salt is harvested → p. 58

● *Sand and more sand*

Beaches as far as the eye can see are one of the Atlantic coast's most memorable features. Sand *en masse* can be found near Arcachon at the *Dune du Pilat*. Towering more than 100m (330ft) over the surrounding area, Europe's highest wandering dune has created a unique landscape along the shore (photo) → p. 68

● *Lighthouses*

Heavy seas on the Atlantic have made life difficult for many a ship's captain since time immemorial. As a consequence, the area has more than its fair share of lighthouses. Climb to the top of the *Phare du Cordouan* at the mouth of the Gironde – the only manned lighthouse left in France → p. 83

● *White horses*

In the south, huge waves roll in from the Atlantic. Hossegor in particular is a *paradise for surfers*. Book a course at the surfing school and try your luck – or lie back in your deckchair and watch others struggling to keep their balance → p. 92

● *Desserts and cheese platters*

Every town has its own delicious desserts and every region its own traditional cheese specialities, ranging from creamy goat's cheese to spicy blue cheese that turn a picnic into a feast. Sample them yourself – e.g. the almond *macarons basques* in and around Saint-Jean-de-Luz or take a look at the variety of cheese in the *Fromagerie Beillevaire* in Nantes → p. 25, 42

ONLY IN

BEST OF ...

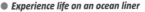

● *Experience life on an ocean liner*
The *Escal'Atlantic museum* in Saint-Nazaire is an exciting place to visit. Even when it's wet you feel like you're on board a luxury liner cruising in the sun. Explore the different decks and soak up the history of transatlantic passenger ships (photo) → p. 36

● *Market magic*
Leave your brolly at home and take a walk around the *indoor markets* in Pornic or Saint-Jean-de-Luz and marvel at the different colours and smells! → p. 45, 94

● *Natural goodness*
Water from above the whole day long can spoil things but water all around can put you in a good mood. Treat yourself to a few hours of pampering with seaweed, marine mud and seawater. A good place for your thalassotherapy is *Hélianthal* in Saint-Jean-de-Luz, for example → p. 94

● *Stay as dry as a bone*
You don't have to get your feet wet to explore the fascinating undersea world. Sharks, piranhas and a state-of-the art, interactive presentation ensure children have just as wonderful a time as their parents at the *aquarium in La Rochelle* → p. 54

● *The Isle of Machines*
You will soon forget the bad weather outside when you visit *Nantes' former shipyards*. Mechanical sea monsters and other maritime creatures come to life here → p. 40

● *Wine tasting in Bordeaux*
If you get caught in the rain in Bordeaux, head for the *Maison du Vin* where you can sample the local wines in peace and quiet until the sun comes out again → p. 74

RAIN

RELAX AND CHILL OUT
Take it easy and spoil yourself

● *Herbs and sunlight*

The *Jardin des Plantes* in Nantes with its magnolias, camellias and count-less beds of herbs, is an oasis in this lively city. Find your own quiet corner and enjoy the scent of the flowers and the sound of the birds → **p. 40**

● *Green Venice*

You will only hear birdsong and the sound of the water on a boat trip through the *Marais Poitevin*. Just lean back and let the guide navigate his way through the marshland (photo) → **p. 60**

● *Relax like Monsieur Hulot*

The best place to relax along the coast is on the beach – even when it's as close to the town as it is in Saint-Nazaire. Just do the same as the main character in *Monsieur Hulot's Holiday* that was filmed here – pack your sunshade and airbed and leave the hustle and bustle of the city behind you on the *Plage de Saint-Marc* → **p. 36**

● *With the wind behind you and sun in your face*

The flat west coast of France is perfect for gentle bike rides. Don't try to go fast but take in the view instead. Particularly lovely trips can be enjoyed on the islands, such as on *Noirmoutier*. Bicycles can be hired everywhere. There's not a steep hill in sight but a beautiful coastline and shady woods instead → **p. 58**

● *Dreamy gardens*

Peace and perfection can be found in the *Parc Jardins du Monde* in Royan. Pick your favourite from the Japanese, Mediterranean and English gardens and spend a few hours among the twittering birds and the scent of the flowers → **p. 62**

● *Bathe in Chardonnay – literally*

The combination of wine and thera-peutic applications at the spa hotel *Les Sources de Caudalie* in Martillac is bal-sam for the soul – even if it comes at a price → **p. 76**

INTRODUCTION

DISCOVER THE FRENCH ATLANTIC COAST!

Burying your toes in the soft sand you gaze out to where the sea and the sky meet on the horizon. Land yachts whiz along the water's edge and the last sun-worshippers of the day shake the sand from their towels. The clatter of crockery can be heard in the restaurants above the beach where shellfish will soon be piled up high on the *étagère* and bottles of chilled white wine uncorked. The proverbial *savoir-vivre* of the French is one of the biggest plus points of any holiday on the Atlantic coast. And the country and the countryside will take care of everything else – seemingly endless beaches, clean water, idyllic fishing villages, historical towns and, last but certainly not least, the 500 wine-producing châteaux around Bordeaux.

Variety is the name of the game in this region that stretches from the south of Brittany down across the broad, flat marshlands of the Vendée to the pine forests of the Landes département and the rocky coastline of the Basque Country. The first jewel in the long chain of beach resorts is La Baule, a traditional seaside town with a wonderful beach, beautiful old villas and a picture-postcard casino. The islands of Noirmoutier

Photo: Port-Vieux beach in Biarritz

In the evening the harbour at Saint-Martin-de-Ré is a paradise for lovers of fresh *fruits de mer*

and Yeu further south form part of the adjoining Côte de Lumière. There are no high-rise blocks here, but wide beaches and a dense network of cycle paths instead, with pretty hibiscus bushes flowering outside every holiday house and small hotel.

For those who love islands, Île de Ré and Île d'Oléron near La Rochelle are two further places to explore where *tout Paris* congregates in summer – especially in the case of Île de Ré. Long bridges and causeways – to Noirmoutier, for example – make them easily accessible. Exquisite villas lie hidden among the trees, most of them the summer houses of wealthy Parisians. And they come here for a very good reason. The islands, with their unspoilt countryside, salt pans and lovely coastlines have a range of gastronomic delights that is on a par with anything in the capital.

The Côte d'Argent lies on the far side of the Gironde estuary, with its endless strip of wide, sandy beaches, forests and seaside lakes so characteristic of *les Landes*. The Landes region, that starts to the south of the Bassin d'Arcachon – a small inland sea

offering all sorts of watersports – is sparsely populated. There are only 88 inhabitants per square mile – as opposed to the national average of more than 260. This is a flat and huge swathe of countryside where riders and cyclists will find hundreds of miles of bridleways and paths. Many cut through the coastal forests that were planted to stop the wind and the 'migrating' dunes from encroaching on the countryside. The result is the largest forested area in Europe covering more than 3800mi². The different varieties of pines are not just attractive – they are also an important economic factor today on the Côte d'Argent.

South of Capbreton and Hossegor the landscape is different yet again. The Côte Basque is a world of its own: rugged cliffs, the elegant resort of Biarritz favoured by surfers and the jet set, the exceptionally pretty little harbour town of Saint-Jean-de-Luz, the Pyrenees rising up behind, a (second) language that is so utterly different from French and an ancient culture that prides itself in its archaic sports – this is the Basque Country where men hurl tree trunks and test their strength chopping wood.

The trading centres of Nantes, La Rochelle and Bordeaux are either on or relatively near the coast and have any number of cultural and historical sights as well as a range of entertainment and shopping

Endless beaches and clean water

facilities expected of larger cities. All three owe a considerable portion of their wealth to the slave trade. Glittery trinkets were loaded onto ships in their ports to be exchanged for people in West Africa who were then transported to the Caribbean to be sold. The ships returned to their home ports laden with indigo dye, coffee, sugar and cocoa.

1562–1598
The wars of religion bring France to its knees.
1598: the Edict of Nantes – Protestant Huguenots are no longer to be persecuted

1643–1715
Cultural and economic heyday under Louis XIV, the Sun King

1789–99
French Revolution. The liberal Girondists from the department of Gironde gain popularity at first but fall victim to the guillotine of the radical Jacobins. Resistance in Royalist Vendée

1914
Bordeaux becomes the seat of the French government in World War I

The money that such freight brought with it was used to build magnificent palatial buildings.

The old cities however also have a sporting and innovative spirit. Bordeaux's football club, Girondins de Bordeaux, has been top of the league six times and the city will be one of the venues for the European Championships in 2016. And Nantes has not only survived the demise of the shipbuilding industry and structural changes –

The home of the most famous red wines in the world

France's sixth largest city and the biggest on the Atlantic coast has also earned itself the title of the European Green Capital 2013, in recognition of successfully combining its economic growth on the one hand with environmental issues and a high standard of living on the other.

It was the Romans who first settled here almost 2000 years ago. But even if they did call the southwest coast of Gaul 'Aquitaine' – from *aqua* – not everything here has to do with water. After all, it was the Romans themselves who showed the locals how to make wine from grapes – a circumstance that was to mark the history of this area and the everyday life of those living here for evermore. Trading in wine on a large scale had its beginnings in Bordeaux and brought the city its prosperity – still very much reflected in the architecture of the historic city centre that has since been carefully restored and was declared a Unesco World Heritage Site in 2007.

The Gironde, the largest estuary of its kind in Europe, forms a wide opening into the Atlantic between Royan and Soulac-sur-Mer, as if it were an arm of the sea itself. The incoming tide reaches 100km (62mi) inland up the Gironde. Médoc, along the west bank, is home to some of the most famous red wines in the world. And of course, this wouldn't be France if the locals weren't also experts in preparing food to match. Fish and seafood characterise menus on the coast, with coveted delights in the form of the controversial *foie gras* or duck breast found further inland.

Despite glamourous seaside resorts such as Royan, Arcachon and Biarritz, the French Atlantic Coast is more down-to-earth than most stretches of the Mediterranean.

1940
Bordeaux briefly becomes the seat of the war-time seat of the French government

2007
Ségolène Royal, president of the Poitou-Charentes Regional Council, stands for the French Socialist Party at the presidential election but loses to Nicolas Sarkozy

2008–2011
Oyster farmers lose between 40–100% of their first and second-year spats to a mysterious epidemic

2016
The European Football Championship to be held in France: the only venue west of Paris is Bordeaux

Thanks to the Dune of Pilat, the Atlantic coast boasts an internationally renowned paragliding spot

Campsites lie cheek by jowl behind the dunes the length of the Côte d'Argent and the banks of inland lakes are perfect for families with children. Prices here are also much more family-friendly than between say Saint-Tropez and Nice.

And with some 500km (310mi) of beach it is not difficult to imagine why the Atlantic coast is a paradise for sport-minded holidaymakers. Waves, sand and wind create perfect conditions for surfing, (land) yachting and paragliding. Thanks to the rivers

Variety draws holidaymakers back to the Atlantic

and lakes, rafting enthusiasts, anglers and the boating fraternity do not miss out either, and those who are wary of the power of the Atlantic will find safer places to swim in the lakes on the Côte d'Argent. Many of these are linked by *courants* – watercourses – and resorts can be found along their banks with holiday houses, campsites, small hotels and a comprehensive range of sport and leisure facilities.

It is this variety that draws many holidaymakers back to the Atlantic time and again. And somewhere along this stretch of coastline, with the sand between your toes and fresh seafood on your plate, you're bound to think of the proverbial *savoir-vivre* of the French. And you'll have to agree, there's certainly some truth to that!

WHAT'S HOT

① Wakeskating

Sport Surfing is passé – nowadays you take to the waves to wakeskate. It's rather like waterskiing but without the binding. Those new to the sport should contact the *Lacanau Wake Center (41, Avenue de la Grande Escoure, lacanaukite-wakecenter.com)* in Lacanau or the *Wakeskate Camp (www.wakelagoona.com)* run by Laurent Delacroix near Bordeaux. Several wake shops even have their own teams such as *Vikteam (305 bis, Avenue d'Eysines, Le Bouscat, www.vikteam.fr)*.

Revues

②

Musical theatres Cabaret is celebrating a revival with lots of glitter and feathers, sensuality and comedy. Colourful spectacles can be enjoyed at *Le Saint Sabastien (11, Rue Charles Plumeau, Couquèques, www.saintsabastien.com, photo)* and in *Caesar's (170, Cours du Médoc, Bordeaux)*. The artistes at *Les Années Boum (Moulin de Bagat, Route de Peyrehorade, Saint-Lon-les-Mines, www.anneesboum.com)* bring a smile to everyone's face with their jazzy costumes, music and dance routines.

Sitting pretty

③

Au revoir verneer France's furniture makers are focussing on a revolutionary and environmentally-friendly material. The creative minded are recycling paper and cardboard to make tables, chairs and cupboards. *Dominique Halimi (14, Cité de Lisbonnes, Bordeaux)* has whacky ideas for storage objects made of cardboard. The range of things you can make out of this material can be seen on the *100% Carton* blog *(www.centpourcentkarton blogspot.com)*. Those who want to get to know the ropes that much better can learn how to make furniture from cardboard at *Singular't (2–4, Rue Darrichon, assosingulart.monsite-orange.fr)* in Biarritz.

RECYCLE

Fish toes

Skin deep Everyone knows the little cleaner fish who live alongside their larger friends in the sea and feed on their parasites and dead scales. The latest beauty fad runs on the same lines too. If you have a fish pedicure, little fish gently and diligently work away at your feet. The tiny nibblers have long been used in medical treatment to help those with skin problems like neurodermatitis. Such pedicures are available in Bordeaux in *Guily Fish Spa (18, Rue des Bahutiers, www.guily-spa.com, photo)* and in *Fish Spa (7, Rue Huguerie)*. At the *L'Institut des Soins du Monde (Place du Général Leclerc)* in Anglet you can even enjoy a treatment session in pairs.

A cut above the rest

Fashion Perfect cuts are the trademark of France's new fashion designers. Marie Rebérat folds, drapes and combines brightly coloured materials. In her boutique in Nantes *(2, Rue Gretry, www.marie-reberat.com)* the designer also sells creations from other colleagues. Bordeaux's leading figure *Laurie-Anne Fritz (12, Rue du Bosquet, laurieannefritz.com)* is also into pleats, plissés and ruches. Her creations are very wearable despite their extravagance. In the *Petit Salon de la Mode (Cité Mondiale du Vin, 18, Par-vis des Chartrons, Bordeaux, www.lepetitsalondelamode.com, photo)* everything revolves around fashion. This is where local shooting stars display what they are working on at the moment. Fashion shows and the direct contact to dozens of creative people whet the appetite much more for contemporary fashion.

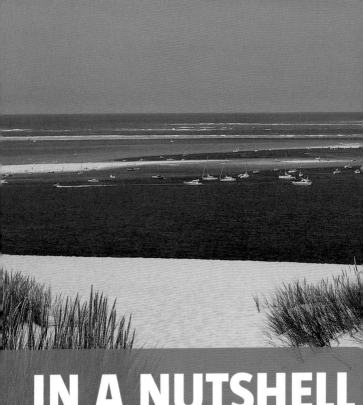

IN A NUTSHELL

A IRBUS
Even if the completion of the A 380 took much longer than planned, the people on the Côte d'Amour love to bask in the fame brought by the giant jumbo. The aircraft manufacturer Airbus plays an important role in this. First and foremost there is the workforce of around 2300 in Saint-Nazaire and a further 2000 in Nantes that gave the economically hard-hit region a decisive new impulse after the demise of the shipbuilding industry. Regular guided tours are offered to tourists in the summer in Saint-Nazaire. The French Atlantic Coast has always been closely associated with flying. Back in the 1930s, seaplanes were tested on the Côte d'Argent.

B ASQUES
250,000 Basques live in the Pays Basque region in the southwest corner of France and 2.5 million in the north of Spain. They share a unique language, *Euskara*, that is considered the oldest in Europe. Although there are concerted efforts to promote the language – all signs in the Basque Country for example are in two languages – its survival is still threatened. Not even half the Basques can speak it and it is not taught everywhere in the region. Basque traditions such as the game

Photo: Dune du Pilat and Banc d'Arguin

Fresh oysters, water, salt and the sea: the cornerstones of life on the French Atlantic Coast

pelota and archaic tests of strength however are carefully upheld, as is Basque architecture. Unlike their fellow countrymen in Spain, the French Basques are not striving for their own independent country but are firmly rooted in France.

COURSE LANDAISE

The battle of wits between man and cow that is very much part of the living folklore of *les Landes*, calls for courage and skill, at least on the part of the *torero*. If at the end of this test of strength one of the two parties is injured – or even dead – then, in a *course landaise*, it's the *torero*. He may have a padded pair of trousers, waistcoat and jacket but he is unarmed and has to try to leap out of the way of the charging cow at the latest possible moment. The aim of the game is to demonstrate one's fearlessness and dexterity. There are 150 arenas along the coast and further inland and, between March and October, they are bursting at the seams at weekends. For forthcoming events, see: *www.courselandaise.org*.

ELEANOR OF AQUITAINE

You'll come across this lady, known as Aliénor d'Aquitaine in French, time and again on this stretch of coastline. Hotels, restaurants and streets have been named after her and she is a firm fixture on every tourist guide's list. Eleanor (c. 1122–1204) inherited the Duchy of Aquitaine, became Queen Consort of France and England and was perhaps the most dazzling female personality of the Middle Ages. Her biography was correspondingly dramatic and it unfurled on this coast. As no son was born while she was Louis VII's wife, the marriage was annulled in 1152. That same year she married Henry Plantagenet, the Count of Anjou and Duke of Normandy, who was to become King Henry II of England. Together the two held sway over Southwest France and England. But these two were also at loggerheads. Henry had numerous affairs while Eleanor held her own court in Poitiers. Under her influence, her sons rose up against their father. Henry crushed the rebellion and had Eleanor imprisoned. It wasn't until after his death in 1189 that she came to power once again, holding onto it until she died in 1204.

O

Of course, apart from wine, water plays a vitally important role in a region, a large part of which has been known since Roman times as *Aquitaine*. This has led to lots of trendy bars and restaurants being given the name 'O' – the text message abbreviation for *eau*, water. And this is where the 'in' crowd can often be found too – in Biarritz, for example.

OYSTERS

Oysters – in other areas they are a luxury; on the Atlantic coast they are part of everyday life. They are both the passion of those living on the coast as well as an economic factor. The French slurp 110,000 tonnes of oysters year for year. When the oyster beds are covered by water at high tide, it is the *cabanes* that characterise the coastline – huts used by farmers for handling the oysters and where you can often buy the freshest (and cheapest). Apart from their being carefully looked after and handled, the quality and temperature of the water play the most important role in perfecting the taste of the shellfish. Oysters from Marennes-Oléron near La Rochelle – the richest oyster beds in Europe yielding 40,000 tonnes – and from the Bassin d'Arcachon, where the water temperature and the blend of salt and fresh water are near perfect, are among the best. The tide also contributes to their quality. Oysters close at low tide. The farmers then climb into the beds to turn the sacks in which the oysters grow – the ones lower down grow more slowly. When the tide is in, the oysters open to feed. It takes between three and four years before an oyster lands on a plate. Up until then, the oyster breeders will have hauled them out of the water up to 20 times, cleaned, sorted and put them back in the oyster beds again. They taste best raw or with a tiny bit of lemon juice.

In summer 2008, a mysterious epidemic decimated a large percentage of the oysters within just a few days. One and two year-old spats were particularly badly effected. The oyster crisis has still not been banished. Viruses and bacteria take their toll on the shellfish and destroy stocks. One of the reasons is the rising temperature in the Atlantic along the coast. Environmental pollution is another possible cause of illness. As oysters do

Pilgrims on the Way of St James at Saint-Jean-Pied-de-Port in the Pyrenees

not have an immune system and cannot be treated, the oyster breeders on the Atlantic, who number just less than 4000, can do little but wait. For many, their very existence is endangered. Consumers however are not effected as imported oysters make up for the missing quantity. The disease killing the oysters has led to the spread of a new form of criminality: the stealing on a massive scale of healthy shellfish from oyster beds that are then sold to restaurants along the coast.

PÊCHE-À-PIED

● Every day at low tide a huge platter of seafood is left on the beach. A mixed bunch of locals and holidaymakers turns up with shovels, rakes and buckets to pick up the mussels, oysters and little crabs for dinner. Check with the tourist information office first about the minimum size of the individual species that you can legally take!

RUGBY

On the Atlantic coast a ball is not always round when it comes to the most beloved pastime in the world. Here, rugby is very much a firm favourite. Many cities in the southwest have successful rugby teams such as the Stade Nantais Université Club, the Union Bordeaux Bègles, Atlantique Stade Rochelais and Biarritz Olympique. Many members of the national team are from Biarritz Olympique. This doesn't mean of course that people are not passionate about football on the Atlantic – but you have until summer 2016 to practice your pronunciation of 'Allez, les Bleus'!

SALT PONDS

Marais salants, salt evaporation ponds, once stretched all the way from southern Brittany to the Gironde estuary. When the sea retreated over the centuries, the ponds became marshland. Today, salt is once again harvested along the coast. Spicy variants and the exquisite *fleur de sel* that forms a wafer-thin layer on the surface of the water on hot days and is scooped up using a wooden shovel, is highly valued by gourmets. The salt ponds have channels that feed saltwater inland into flat pans called *aires* that are at slightly different levels. The water, regulated by sluice gates, flows from one pan to the next. A pink coloured crystalline layer forms on the surface which turns white when dry. The small crystals on the surface form a core around which larger crystals of grey salt are created. This is piled up in the middle of the pan so that surplus water can drain before being shaped into the characteristic pyramid-like mounds around the edge of the salt works, as can be seen in the Vendée and on Noirmoutier and Ré.

THALASSOTHERAPY

Thalassotherapy – saltwater therapy – can be found in most resorts along the Atlantic coast. If you want to do things properly, you'll need to invest at least one

BOOKS & FILMS

▶ **Georges Simenon** – The Atlantic coast, especially the Côte de Lumière, has inspired many a writer. Georges Simenon (1903–89), who invented the detective Maigret, loved the Vendée and La Rochelle. 15 of his novels are set in the port including *The Hatter's Ghost*. Les Sables-d'Olonne provides the backdrop for *Maigret on Holiday*

▶ **Under the Sand** – Charlotte Rampling stars in this drama directed and written by François Ozon about loss, bereavement and life's delusions, as a woman whose husbands goes for a swim and never returns

▶ **Pauline at the Beach** – This film from 1982 by Éric Rohmer, which is not without its funny side, tells of the teenager's amorous adventures and those of her older cousin, Marion, on the Atlantic coast

▶ **Monsieur Hulot's Holiday** – The classic comedy from 1953, directed by Jacques Tati, is essential viewing before any trip to the Atlantic coast. The film does with little use of language and conjures up a wonderful holiday atmosphere

▶ **Little White Lies** – The wind blowing in off the Atlantic coast can be felt in Guillaume Canet's comedy-drama film made in 2010 about a group of friends and couples on their summer holiday in Arcachon. Funny and sad, jovial and melancholy, amusing and never boring – *très français* in fact

▶ **Eleanor of Aquitaine: By the Wrath of God, Queen of England** – The author, Alison Weir, has produced a carefully researched, vivid biography which throws a new and provocative light on arguably the most extraordinary woman in the Middle Ages.

week, with half of each day being taken up with therapy sessions including water gymnastics, saltwater jacuzzis, massage jet showers, algae paste and fango packs. But even without a medical reason, a day of thalassotherapy is good for the body and soul. It relieves backache, helps the respiratory system and skin problems, rheumatism and stress-related symptoms as well as improving one's general sense of well-being. Sun and sea air do their bit too.

THE WAY OF ST JAMES

For more than 1000 years pilgrims have been making their way to Santiago de Compostela in Spain where Saint James is reputedly buried. The scallop shell, that has been the traditional emblem of Saint James since the 11th century, can be seen in many churches in Aquitaine. One of the four main pilgrim routes through France that converge in the Pyrenees, leads from Soulac-sur-Mer at the mouth of the Gironde, down the Atlantic coast to Saint-Jean-de-Luz. The coastal route, also known as the 'English Path' as it was popular among the British as well as the Dutch and Bretons, is the most direct route to the Pyrenees. 550km (342mi) have now been made into a cycle path.

WINE

Wine has been grown in the southwest of France since Roman times. After the decline of the Roman Empire it was the monks who kept the happy memory of grape juice alive. Viniculture experienced a big boom following the marriage of Eleanor of Aquitaine with Henry Plantagenet. Through this union a brisk trade was established with England and the Hanseatic League, from which Bordeaux and Bayonne profited in particular. Today, some 8000 châteaux around

Bordeaux alone – many of the wineries being of a princely dimension – ensure that, at least here, you're going to be pushed for time if you want to sample as many different wines as possible. Bordelais produces 700 million bottles a year, making it the largest wine-growing area in the world. First-class wines from the Bordeaux

In Saint-Émilion the cellar is the belle étage: Château Franc Mayne

area known throughout the world include the five *premiers crus classés* from the Médoc region's 1500 châteaux: Château Lafite-Rothschild, Château Latour and Château Mouton-Rothschild in Pauillac as well as, slightly further south, Château Margaux and Château Haut-Brion. The scenic Médoc and Haut-Médoc area lies along the banks of the Gironde estuary.

FOOD & DRINK

In France, cooking is considered an art and the production of food a craft that does not tolerate compromises. Apart from the large supermarkets with their first-class fish, meat and cheese counters, traditional bakeries, cake shops, fish, vegetable and cheese specialists and *chocolatiers* all still hold their own.

Everything revolves around fresh, unadulterated ingredients, preferably locally sourced. The range of food is dominated by fish and seafood on the coast. The further inland you go, the heartier the dishes – from braised eel to *cassoulet*, a rich casserole from the Périgord region that is given its special flavour by adding duck *confit*. Apart from duck or goose *foie gras* and tender duck breast *(magret de canard)*, leg of duck *(cuisses)* and duck fillets *(aiguillettes)* are also frequently served. Even the fat and giblets are cooked, such as gizzards *(gésiers de canard)*. The tender aromatic flesh is a tasty addition to salads.

Bordeaux is famous for its cep mushrooms that are used in omelettes or served with entrecôtes. Cattle with a particularly tender and tasty meat are bred in Bazas and *les Landes*. Truffles from Périgord known as Black Diamonds are a speciality that comes at a price, as it has not been possible so far to cultivate them on farms.

Oysters, duck and world-class wine: fish and seafood are very much in evidence on the coast as are more hearty dishes further inland

Fortunately, just a couple of pieces of a few ounces suffice to give poultry dishes or omelettes that incomparable aroma.

Regional confectionery specialists have a whole range of calorie-rich nibbles at the ready. Try *mascarons nantais*, light chocolate creations from Nantes, as well as *rigolettes* that also come from the city on the Loire, *canelés* from Bordeaux, little vanilla pastries with a caramelized crust, and ● *macarons basques*, almond macaroons from the far southwest.

The culinary start to the day is light – and sweet. Breakfast in hotels and in cafés usually comprises white coffee *(café crème)* with croissants, baguette, butter and marmalade. Supplementing a classic breakfast with ham, a selection of cheese and fruit is no longer anything unusual in medium category hotels. Many

LOCAL SPECIALITIES

▶ **agneau de pré-salé** – especially aromatic lamb grazed on the salt marshes in the Vendée

▶ **bordelaise, à la** – with shallots, tarragon and red wine sauce, e.g. entrecôte

▶ **brébis (des Pyrénées)** – sheep's cheese (from the Pyrenees)

▶ **chipirons (à l'encre)** – squid (in its own ink)

▶ **confit de canard** – duck preserved in its own fat (photo above right)

▶ **coquilles Saint-Jacques** – scallops

▶ **garbure** – cabbage soup with meat

▶ **gâteau basque** – plain flan-like cake from the Basque Country

▶ **huîtres** – oysters; the most common are the *fine de claire* variety from oyster farms (photo above left)

▶ **jambon de Bayonne** – air-dried ham from Bayonne

▶ **landaise, à la** – prepared to a recipe from *les Landes* region: with garlic and pine nuts sautéed in duck lard

▶ **loukinkos** – Basque garlic sausage

▶ **marmitako** – Basque tuna ragout

▶ **mouclade** – mussels in a thick white-wine and yolk sauce, sometimes with curry powder

▶ **pipérade** – Basque omelette with peppers and tomatoes

▶ **plateau de fruits de mer** – raw – mussels *(coquillages)* and oysters *(huîtres)* and – cooked – shrimps *(crevettes)*, salt water snails *(bulots* and *bigorneaux)*, spider crabs *(araignée de mer)*, brown crabs *(tourteau)* – seafood and shellfish on a large platter, the more luxurious variations being with lobster *(homard)* or crayfish *(langouste)*

▶ **salmis** – ragout in a spicy sauce, e.g. *canard* (duck) or *palombe* (pigeon)

▶ **ttoro** – Basque fish soup with tomatoes and peppers

hotels down the coast have also expanded their menus to include a variety of egg dishes to please guests from north of the Channel. *Moules frites*, mussels and chips, are popular at lunchtime and you will always find a *steak frites* and salads with and without seafood on the menu too. Bars and *brasseries* have a variety of baguette sandwiches for a quick snack as well as toasted bread (not baguette) with cheese and ham. Half or a full dozen oysters – eaten in the evening more as an *hors d'œuvre* – can be found all down the coast, and they are cheap too! They are usually served raw or with a zest of lemon at the most before separating them from their shell with a fork and slurping them down.

The most important meal of the day in France is *dîner* that is served between 7pm–9.30pm. It usually consists of several courses and wine is always served regardless of whether you're in a run-of-the-mill restaurant on the harbourside or in a gourmet temple. The first course is generally seafood. But those who don't like fish won't have to go hungry – there are also pastries with herbs, soups and salads, *foie gras* from fattened geese (*d'oie*) and duck (*de canard*) – and snails. The main course could by a perfectly cooked entrecôte (*saignant,* rare, *à point,* medium, or *bien cuit,* well done), lamb, eel braised in red wine or Cognac or *poisson du jour,* fish of the day – either from the ocean or from a lake.

You have a choice from a whole range of delicious goat's cheeses afterwards, including various blue cheeses and regional specialities such as Jonchée, a cream cheese made from cow's milk produced around Rochefort. Then there are the sweet temptations: classics such as *mousse au chocolat* or local delicacies like *broyé du Poitou,* a crisp biscuity cake sprinkled with flaked almonds that is not as light as it looks due to all the butter in it. Finally, Cognac is served as a *digestif.*

The most important drink at mealtimes in this region is, of course, wine, preferably from Bordelais. The famous reds (clarets) are produced in Médoc and Saint-Émilion; excellent whites in the Loire valley and the Entre-Deux-Mers region southeast of Bordeaux. In the case of whites, the sweet wines should also be mentioned here that are the perfect accompaniment to desserts and cheese, but also unfurl their full flavour with *foie gras.* The most famous is Sauternes that is made from the Sémillon grape harvested late in the season.

Pineau, in particular, from the Poitou-Charentes region, has become a popular *apéritif.* It comprises three-quarters sweet grapejuice and one-quarter Cognac. It can also be served as a tasty dessert wine with melon or another fruit, for example. White Pineau is drier; Pineau rosé is fruitier. The Cognac region near Royan covers 310mi² and reaches as far as the Atlantic coast. Cognac is generally served after a meal but is gaining popularity as an *apéritif.*

Typical of the Basque Pyrenees: the Espelette pepper

SHOPPING

Looking around and shopping at the colourful markets, in pretty shops or at wine-producers' themselves are a real pleasure. Normal opening hours are Mon–Sat 10am–7pm. In villages and small towns most things close for a lunch break; in the holiday resorts boutiques and shops usually stay open all day and are often open longer in the evenings and on Sundays too. Evening markets (7pm–10pm) are held along the coast in the high season, selling crafts, local specialities and clothes. Antique shops are also well worth visiting as are craft workshops. Things may not be cheap but are unusual and well made.

CHILDREN'S CLOTHES

Children's clothes in France are often cheaper, more imaginatively designed and prettier than in many other countries. Certain brand names considered exclusive outside France are quite normal here, e.g. children's underclothing from Petit Bateau is not only sold in boutiques but also in department stores like Monoprix and *hypermarchés* such as Leclerc – and that can be seen in the prices. The Du Pareil au Même (DPAM) label, e.g. in Nantes, Saint-Nazaire, La Rochelle and Bordeaux, is very popular and good value.

FASHION

Most Parisian fashion labels can also be found in the coastal towns and in Nantes, La Rochelle and Bordeaux, although prices are not necessarily any lower. Summer sales however still exist in France – and from around the beginning of the school holidays real bargains can be found. In surfer eldorados such as Hossegor and Biarritz you can deck yourself out with brightly-coloured sportswear. Surfing gear and leisurewear such as hoodies, jeans and fleeces from the Australian brand Billabong (which has its European headquarters in Hossegor) or flip-flops from Ipanema can be found in boutiques near the beach everywhere.

FOOD

Shopping and food go hand in hand on the Atlantic coast. The markets and fantastic delicatessens make sure of that. And

At the market or the wine-maker's – here you'll find a wide range of things for your wardrobe, larder or cellar

not only chocoholics will feel they are in heaven at a *chocolatier*. Handmade chocolate may not be a very suitable souvenir in summer but it is all the more enjoyable on the spot. Coarse sea salt or the fine-grained delicate *fleur de sel* from the salt farms on the Guérande peninsula or from one of the islands on the other hand is easy to transport.

KITCHEN ACCESSORIES

Things for the kitchen also make nice souvenirs, from china egg-cups and coffee bowls with maritime patterns to tea towels and aprons – with Breton motifs in the north or traditional bright stripes on the Côte Basque. These stripes also decorate tablecloths, napkins and cushion covers and can be found in boutiques in Biarritz, Bayonne and Saint-Jean-de-Luz, as well as in many villages in the Basque Country.

MUSIC

When in a CD shop in Bordeaux, look out for the independent label 'Vicious Circle' that promotes local artists including the band Calc. Melanie Valera, originally from Bordeaux, is also one of the company's discoveries. In the past few year she has brought out a number of electropop albums under her performing name 'Tender Forever'. These are distributed in France by Vicious Circle. These albums keep their magic long after your holiday is over.

WINES & SPIRITS

You can try wine at wine producers' and then fill up your boot. Excellent wines can be found in the Loire Valley, in Bordelais, Pineau des Charentes and Cognac in the Charente area inland from the Côte de Lumière.

THE PERFECT ROUTE

FROM NANTES TO NOIRMOUTIER

In ① *Nantes* → p. 38 you can find out everything about the region where world history was written in the Middle Ages in the Château des Ducs de Bretagne. Treat yourself to a romantic trip on the River Erdre and then take the road via ② *Saint-Nazaire* → p. 36, where the Loire meets the Atlantic, down the coast to ③ *Île de Noirmoutier* → p. 58. *En route*, it is worth stopping at the pretty fishing town ④ *Pornic* → p. 43 (photo left). A relaxing time awaits you on Noirmoutier: cycling and sunbathing as well as delicious seafood.

THE PICTURESQUE ISLAND OF OLÉRON

Then it's off down the coast, pausing a while in the pretty resort ⑤ *Saint-Gilles-Croix-de-Vie* → p. 61. It is worth spending at least one day in the beautiful and lively port ⑥ *La Rochelle* → p. 53 (photo right), exploring the bustling Old Town, the market and visiting the aquarium, before going on to ⑦ *Oléron* → p. 47. Beaches, little harbours and masses of unspoilt countryside are a guarantee for a peaceful holiday.

WATER AND WINE: MÉDOC

Back on the mainland, cross from Royan to the Médoc peninsula and head for ⑧ *Pauillac* → p. 80, home to one of the most famous châteaux in the world. Book a wine tasting session through a tourist information office at one château at least. Apart from top wines, the peninsula also has a number of watersports facilities and interesting excursions to offer such as to the ⑨ *Phare de Cordouan* → p. 83, so that several days can easily be spent here.

ENDLESS BEACHES

Once you have found your favourite Bordeaux red, the next stretch of your journey focuses entirely on the ocean. Leaving Bordeaux behind you for the time being, you will reach the traditional seaside resort ⑩ *Arcachon* → p. 65. The ⑪ *Dune du Pilat* → p. 68, a unique natural phenomenon, rises up just beyond the town. Follow the Côte d'Argent

Experience the different facets of the French Atlantic Coast from north to south with detours to the islands

southwards, passing through the quiet beachside resorts ⑫ *Biscarrosse → p. 68* and ⑬ *Mimizan → p. 77*. A lovely place to complete this stretch of the route is ⑭ *Capbreton → p. 91*.

HUGE WAVES ON THE BASQUE COAST

After the endlessly wide beaches of the 'Silver Coast', the French Basque Country is twisty and rugged but with wonderful bays and beaches in between. Stop off for a bit of culture in ⑮ *Bayonne → p. 90* that is famous for its half-timbered buildings and delicious chocolate, before visiting glamourous ⑯ *Biarritz → p. 84* down the road. Apart from the wonderful beaches and enormous breakers, you will find a beautiful Old Town and excellent shopping. And don't miss the idyllic seaside resort and fishing village ⑰ *Saint-Jean-de-Luz → p. 92*, just a few miles further south.

A DETOUR INLAND

The return journey takes you inland through the extensive pine forests of *les Landes*. The first port of call is ⑱ *Dax → p. 91* that can be reached on the A 63 motorway. In France's oldest spa you can found out why this area has been called Aquitaine since Roman times. In mid August, the arena is packed for bullfights.

BORDEAUX AND SAINT-ÉMILION

⑲ *Bordeaux → p. 71* has exciting museums, elegant shops and the gastronomic delights of a flamboyant city. A detour to ⑳ *Saint-Émilion → p. 77* is certainly worthwhile. This little old town is in a wonderful setting and is not just appealing to wine-lovers.

Approx. 1150km (715mi), incl. detours.
Recommended time: at least 2, preferably 3 weeks. Detailed map of the route on the back cover, in the road atlas and the pull-out map

CÔTE D'AMOUR

Historically speaking, this section of the French Atlantic Coast belonged to Southern Brittany for many centuries.
Today, the département Loire-Atlantique comes under the administration of the Pays-de-la-Loire region, but the Breton heritage is still very much alive in the minds of the locals with the words *en Bretagne* scrawled onto signs in many towns and villages. Apart from Nantes, which was once the capital of Brittany and now of the Pays-de-la-Loire, the traditional resort La Baule and the port Saint-Nazaire also belong to the same region. Salt has been harvested on the Guérande peninsula for centuries, as is the case in the Vendée and on the Côte de Lumière. It is gathered between June and September, but the salt evaporation ponds can be visited the whole year round. The Côte d'Amour is also known for its idyllic fishing villages sheltered in rocky coves. The strip of coast beyond the Loire estuary is called the Côte de Jade. It reaches from Pointe de Saint-Gildas – a rocky headland – down to Pornic.

LA BAULE

(128 A2) (*ⓜ A3*) ★ **This traditional little town (pop. 17,000) located on the Guérande peninsula evolved into a sea-**

Photo: La Baule beach

Rocky bays and fishing villages, a fashionable seaside resort and the salt ponds around Guérande – this stretch of coast is full of variety

side resort at the beginning of the 20th century when wealthy Parisians had villas built similar to those in spas in Normandy. A stroll past the villas from the 1880s to the 1950s is like a quick *tour de France*, with houses in the style of the Basque Country, Normandy and Provence lining the lovely bay. And of course lots of hotels. 2000 buildings are listed and contribute to the appeal of this town, together with its almost 10km (6¼mi)-long fine sandy beach and an extensive range of leisure and sports facilities.

SIGHTSEEING

MUSÉE AÉRONAUTIQUE PRESQU'ÎLE CÔTE D'AMOUR

Aircraft from the early days of flying up to today. *Aérodrome de la Baule | Mon*

Fishing tackle in the busy harbour in Le Croisic

and Wed–Fri 2pm–5pm | www.mapica.
org

FOOD & DRINK

CASTEL MARIE-LOUISE

Eric Mignard's top-class restaurant with an emphasis on regional fare in the hotel of the same name. The fish in a salt crust is excellent. *Closed at lunchtime except on Sun (July/Aug Sat/Sun), | 1, Avenue Andrieu | tel. 02 40 11 48 38 | www.castel-marie-louise.com | Expensive*

LA CROISETTE

This good-value cosy brasserie is right in the thick of things in the town centre. *Daily | 31, Place du Maréchal Leclerc | tel. 02 40 60 73 00 | www.lacroisette.fr | Budget*

INSIDER TIP LE TAM TAM

Oysters, fish and regional specialities on the beach. The food is more down-to-earth than refined; the service and atmosphere exceptionally good. *Opposite no. 16, Boulevard Darlu | tel. 02 40 24 26 47 | Moderate*

LA VÉRANDA

Sophisticated and imaginative cuisine in the Hotel Bellevue Plage. *Closed Mon lunchtime and Wed, in July/Aug Mon lunchtime only | 27, Boulevard de l'Océan | tel 02 40 60 57 77 | www.restaurant-laveranda com | Expensive*

SHOPPING

There are lots of boutiques in the *Avenue du Général de Gaulle.* The market *(Tue-Sun | Avenue du Marché)* doesn't just offer salt and souvenirs – you can also enjoy fresh oysters with a glass of wine. Try the INSIDER TIP *caramels au beurre salé -* the mixture of sweet caramel and salted butter is irresistible! The world and his wife is here on Sat. A craft market is held on Sun mornings in July and August on the *Avenue des Ibis.*

SPORTS & ACTIVITIES

All the facilities expected of a large seaside resort can be found here, ranging from all types of watersports to cycle

hire and riding. There is a golf course
in La Baule itself and in Guérande, Le
Croisic, Mesquer and Saint-André-des-
Eaux. Thalassotherapy is offered at *Relais
Thalasso La Baule (28, Boulevard de
l'Océan | tel. 02 40 11 33 11 | www.thalasso-
labaule.com)* and *Thalgo La Baule (Avenue
Marie-Louise | tel. 02 40 11 99 99 | www.
thalassobarriere.com).*

ENTERTAINMENT

Popular clubs include *Le Théâtre (10,
Avenue Pavie)* and *L'Indiana Club* in the
casino *(Esplanade Lucien Barrière).*

WHERE TO STAY

HERMITAGE BARRIÈRE

One of the most elegant hotels in the
town – or, rather, on the beach. A heated
seawater pool, sauna and gym mean you
are independent of the weather. *192
rooms | 5, Esplanade Lucien Barrière | tel.
02 40 11 46 46 | www.hermitage-barriere.
com | Expensive*

VILLA CAP D'AIL

Built in 1927 just 100m from the beach,
this villa is typical of La Baule. It has individually furnished rooms and a lovely
garden. *22 rooms | 145, Avenue Maréchal-
de-Lattre-de-Tassigny | tel. 02 40 60 29 30 |
www.villacapdail.com | Moderate*

INFORMATION

*3, Place de la Victoire | tel. 02 40 24 34 44 |
www.labaule.fr*

WHERE TO GO

LE CROISIC (128 A2) (*Ш A3*)

This pretty fishing port and marina (pop.
4600) is a popular holiday destination. It
is located at the end of a peninsula, 10km

(6¼mi) west of La Baule. Although the
coastline and beaches are rocky, sandy
bays are exposed at low tide. The flora and
fauna of the Atlantic can be marvelled at
in the *Océarium du Croisic (Avenue de
Saint-Goustan | June daily 10am–6pm, July/
Aug 10am–7pm, otherwise usually 10am–
noon and 2pm–6pm | www.ocearium-
croisic.fr)* which offers an excitingly presented journey into the undersea world
and can be unreservedly recommended
for families with children.

The elegant hotel and restaurant *Le Fort
de l'Océan (9 rooms | restaurant closed
Mon/Tue Sept–June, Mon–Thu at lunch-
time in July | La Pointe du Croisic | tel. 02 40
15 77 77 | www.fort-ocean.com | Expensive)*

MARCO POLO HIGHLIGHTS

⭐ **The Escal'Atlantic
museum experience in
Saint-Nazaire**
Anyone interested in ships
and travel will have masses
of fun here → p. 36

⭐ **La Baule**
Grand 19th-century and early
20th-century architecture
give this traditional seaside
resort its exceptional charm
→ p. 32

⭐ **Île de Nantes**
An impressive example
of how an industrial area
can be transformed into
a cultural centre → p. 39

⭐ **Pornic**
Beautiful coastal town
on the Côte de Jade with
a harbour and coast
paths with lovely views
→ p. 43

is on the headland at the end of the peninsula. Ferries to the islands Belle-Île, Houat and Hœdic depart from the harbour *(www.compagniedesiles.com)*. Information: *6, Rue du Pilori | tel. 02 40 23 00 70 | www.tourisme-lecroisic.fr*

GUÉRANDE (128 A2) *(m A3)*

The salt capital (pop. 14,000) lies 6km (3¾mi) north of La Baule. The medieval town wall with its towers and gateways is impressive. *Fleur de sel*, the best quality sea salt, is harvested in the salt evaporation ponds. The ponds and exhibition are open to visitors: *Terre de Sel (Route des Marais Salants | Pradel | April/May daily | 10am–12.30pm and 2pm–6pm, June and Sept 10am–6pm, July/Aug 9.30am–8pm, Oct–March 10am–12.30pm and 2pm–5pm | www.terredesel.fr)*. The *Musée du Pays de Guérande* is also very interesting *(Porte Saint-Michel | April–Sept Tue–Sun 10am–12.30pm and daily 2.30pm–7pm, Oct Tue–Sun 10am–noon and daily 2pm–6pm)*. The history of the town and the region is narrated on three floors in one of the three town gateways.

An especially 'green' hotel built using ecologically-sound materials is ☺ *Econuit (70 rooms | 1, Rue du Milan Noir | tel. 02 40 45 85 47 | www.econuit.com | Budget)*. Information: *1, Place du Marché aux Bois | tel. 02 40 24 96 71 | www.ot-guerande.fr*

PARC NATUREL RÉGIONAL DE BRIÈRE (128 A–B2) *(m A–B3)*

Guided boat trips are available through the marshlands of this nature reserve that covers 190mi², starting in Crossac Mine, Bréca or Saint-Lyphard. There are INSIDER TIP two excellent restaurants offering regional specialities (such as eel in a salt crust) in or near *Saint-Lyphard*: *Auberge de Bréca (closed Sun evening and Mon | Bréca | tel. 02 40 91 41 42 | www.auberge-breca.com | Expensive)* and *L'Auberge Les Typhas (closed Wed lunch time and Tue | Rue du Vignonnet | tel. 02 40 91 32 32 | www.leschaumieresdulac. com | Moderate)*. Information: *Village de Kerhinet | Saint-Lyphard | tel. 02 40 66 85 01 | www.parc-naturel-briere.fr*

PIRIAC-SUR-MER (128 A2) *(m A3)*

Artists and writers used to spend their holidays here in the olden days. Today, this little village (pop. 2300) 18km (11mi) to the northwest is an idyllic, family-friendly resort with bays for swimming set against a backdrop of pines. On Thu evenings in summer an art and craft market is held on the Place de l'Église. Information: *7, Rue des Cap-Horniers | tel. 02 40 23 51 42 | www.piriac.net*

PORNICHET (128 A2) *(m A3)*

Family-friendly seaside resort (population 10,000) with three beaches on the eastern side of La Baule Bay. The 4km (2½mi) long *Plage Libraires*, that slopes gently, is particularly popular. The elegant old façades and the casino testify to Pornichet's history as a holiday resort. Thalassotherapy is offered in the *Centre Daniel Jouvance (66, Boulevard des Océanides | tel. 02 40 61 89 98 | www.thalasso-danieljouvance. com)*. Information: *3, Boulevard de la République | tel. 02 40 61 33 33 | www. pornichet.fr*

SAINT-NAZAIRE (128 B2) *(m B3)*

Saint-Nazaire (pop. 69,000) is 14km (8½mi) to the east of La Baule, right on the Loire estuary which is spanned by a spectacular bridge. The town is first and foremost a port, shipyard and home to the Airbus works but also boasts 20 beaches. A statue of Monsieur Hulot on the ● *Plage de Saint-Marc* is a reminder that Jacques Tati made his famous film here in 1953. The fascinating ★ ● *Escal'Atlantic* museum experience *(April–Sept daily, Oct–De-*

and Feb/March Wed–Sun 10am–12.30pm and 2pm–6pm, mid July–Aug 10am–7pm | visit-saint-nazaire.de) in a former submarine base, includes a reproduction of a transatlantic steamer like the ones that left Saint-Nazaire for America in the 1920s and 1930s. Cabins, the bridge and decks have been authentically reconstructed. The harbour was built by the Germans in

is built, among other planes, is a must for aircraft fans. Advanced booking however is required for the tours – which are in French only *(reservations at least 10 days in advance: tel. 02 28 54 06 40 | passports must be shown | visit-saint-nazaire.de)*. In July/August, some tours around the *STX France* shipyard are held in English. Depending on the work in hand, you can

The elegant Pont de Saint-Nazaire spans the wide mouth of the Loire

941 during the occupation of France using a colossal 17,500,000ft³ of cement. Attempts by the Allied Forces to bomb it, resulted in 90% of the town being destroyed. Three chambers inside the bunker have since been turned into rooms for events. The *LIFE* room *(Lieu International des Formes Emergentes)* is now a centre for contemporary art and the *VIP* room has a stage and adjoining bar. The bunker is crowned by a dome that has come from Tempelhof Airport in Berlin and was used to protect the radar unit up until 2003. A visit to the Airbus works *(tel. 02 28 54 06 40)* in the harbour, where the A 380

watch huge passenger ships being assembled in the dry dock from the gallery.
Fresh fish can be enjoyed in the restaurant *La France (Plage de Saint-Marc | tel. 02 40 91 96 27 | www.lefrance.net | Budget)*. Information: *Boulevard de la Légion d'Honneur | Base sous-marine | tel. 02 40 22 40 65 | www.saint-nazaire-tourisme.com*

LA TURBALLE
(128 C3–4) (*ω A3*)
This little fishing village (pop. 3000) 13km (8mi) northwest of La Baule has very much an air of Brittany, a lovely sandy beach and a lively harbour that is famous for

the sardines that are brought to shore here. A fish market is held in the *market hall (Espace Garlahy)* daily in July/August, otherwise Wed and Sat. In July/August it is well worth visiting the evening *arts and crafts market (Wed 7pm–9pm | Quai Saint-Pierre)*. Au Gré des Vents, a sardine cutter built in 1664, can be seen in the museum *La Maison de la Pêche (Port de La Turballe | school holidays Mon–Sat 10am–12.30pm and 2.30pm–6pm, Sun 3pm–6pm | musee-laturballe.fr)*. The history and methods of sardine fishing are explained in a 45-minute guided tour on the fishing boat. Ferries to the Breton islands of Belle-Île, Houat and Hœdic depart from the harbour. Information: *Place Charles de Gaulle | tel. 02 40 23 39 87 | www.tourisme-laturballe.fr*

NANTES

MAP INSIDE BACK COVER
(128–129 C–D3) (*ω* C3–4)
Nantes (pop. 278,000), at one time the capital of Brittany, lies at the confluence of the rivers Loire, Erdre and Sèvre.
In the 18th century Nantes was the most important port in France. The closure of the dockyards in 1987 plunged the city into a period of crisis. In the meantime, a structural change has been successfully accomplished. The Airbus works here and in Saint-Nazaire as well as an expansion in the food processing and metal working industries have contributed to this. Today, Nantes is the administrative centre of the Pays-de-la-Loire region, the sixth largest city and second most important financial centre in France and a university town with a large range of cultural and commercial attractions.

SIGHTSEEING

CATHÉDRALE SAINT-PIERRE-ET-SAINT-PAUL
At 37.5m (123ft) the nave is higher than that of Notre-Dame in Paris. The façade dates from the late Middle Ages; the external pulpit is an unusual feature. The stoups made of shells from the Indian Ocean in the Late Gothic interior are noteworthy, as is the Renaissance tomb (that has been empty since the Revolution) of the last Breton Duke, François II and his wife Marguerite de Foix, made of black-and-white marble. Their daughter Anne, whose portrait has also been chiselled out of marble, became Queen of France and is buried in Saint-Dénis near Paris. Her heart, however, found its final resting place here, in the cathedral *crypt (July/Aug Tue–Sun 3pm–6pm, Sat also 10am–12.30pm, May–June Sat 10am–12.30pm and 3pm–6pm, Sun 3pm–6pm, Sept–April Sat/Sun 3pm–6pm). Place Saint-Pierre*

CHÂTEAU DES DUCS DE BRETAGNE
The seat of the Dukes of Brittany was built from 1466 onwards as a fortress and residence. Following the marriage of Anne de Bretagne with Charles VIII it became the Breton palace of the French royal family. It was rebuilt in the Classicist style after a fire in the 17th century. The ● ⚞ wal

---

CITY WHERE TO START?
Drivers should head for the multi-storey car park on **Place du Commerce** which pedestrians can also reach on trams 1, 2 and 4. The medieval town, the Quartier Graslin cultural district and Île Feydeau with most of the important sights, are within easy walking distance. Trentemoult can be reached by water taxi from Gare Maritime; the Île de Nantes on trams 2 and 3 across the Pont Anne de Bretagne.

long the ramparts and to the towers offers a lovely view of both the Old Town and the new city. The ducal apartments house the *municipal museum (July/Aug daily 10am–7pm, otherwise Tue–Sun 10am–6pm)*, with a multi-media, audiovisual and interactive presentation of the history of Nantes and Brittany. *4, Place Marc Elder*

open to the public. The author spent the first eight years of his life in Nantes. *Allée Duguay Trouin/Quai Turenne*

ÎLE DE NANTES ⭐

Several bridges link the city with the Île de Nantes which is some 5km (3mi) long and 1km (½mi) wide and washed by two

The building of Nantes cathedral took 459 years to complete

ÎLE FEYDEAU

In 1926–42 the lower section of the Erdre and several tributaries of the Loire were filled in, which meant that Île Feydeau – that was shaped like a ship – was no longer an island. In the 18th century, the wide streets and shipowners' villas with their carved mascaron ornamentation (faces) turned this district into the most modern in the city. All the buildings have now been restored. On the edge of the former island, on Cours Olivier de Clisson, a plaque marks the house where Jules Verne (1828–1905) was born. It is not

arms of the Loire. In the olden days it was the centre of the maritime trade and shipbuilding. Since the turn of the millennium it has been planted up – to create the *Parc des Chantiers* among others – and given a new lease of life. A district has evolved that has not only attracted businesses but residents too. Contemporary architecture has found a foothold here as has avant-garde culture that fits in well among relics from the industrial era, such as the crane from the 1960s that is now a listed industrial monument. The island's most popular attraction is the

12m (39ft)-high *Grand Éléphant* that can carry up to 45 people on a ☀ viewing platform on its back. Its mechanical moving parts are fascinating: its ears flap, the trunk moves and even sprays water and it can blink. All its movements are based on those of a living animal. Steered by a driver, the elephant can carry visitors and locals at 4km/h (2½mph) from the banks of the Loire to the machine gallery in a former shipbuilding hangar where mechanical sea monsters congregate as one might expect to find '20,000 leagues under the sea'.

including octopuses, giant fish, a boat whipped by a storm, a coach and horses and sea snakes. Visitors can ride on the machines like on a roundabout and watch them being built in the workshop. The *Mondes Marins,* a 25m (82ft)-high merry go-round opened in 2012 and will be

The *Grand Éléphant* is the star in the weird and wonderful *Machines de l'Île*

The elephant is part of a project ● *Les Machines de l'Île (Boulevard Léon-Bureau | April–June and Sept/Oct Tue–Sun 10am–5pm, July/Aug daily 10am–8pm, Nov/Dec and mid Feb–March Wed–Sun 2pm–5pm | www.lesmachines-nantes.fr),* to which the *Galerie des Machines* also belongs. It comprises a collection of mechanical fantasy creatures in a former shipbuilding hangar,

followed in 2016 by *L'Arbre aux Herons,* a tree of the same height with two larger than-life herons. It will not only be possible to go in it – a café will also be built in its canopy. Plans for the project that are reminiscent of Leonardo da Vinci' drawings can already be seen in the gallery. An exhibition documenting the re development of the island is housed in *Hangar 32 (32, Quai des Antilles | Fri–Sun 2pm–6pm | www.iledenantes.com).*

JARDIN DES PLANTES ●

17 acres bursting with medicinal plants camellias and magnolias. *Entrances on Boulevard Stalingrad and Place Sophie*

Trébuchet | daily 8.30am–8pm, winter until 5.30pm

MUSÉE DES BEAUX ARTS

One of the most beautiful art collections in France with masterpieces by Ingres, Courbet, Chagall, Picasso and Kandinsky. *10, Rue Georges Clémenceau | closed for renovation until early 2014*

MUSÉE JULES VERNE

The villa on the hill Sainte-Anne houses letters by the author who was born in 1828 in Nantes and manuscripts of his famous adventure stories. Next to the museum is a sculpture of Jules Verne as a child sitting quietly on a bench next to Captain Nemo, a figure in his novels, gazing out over the river. Free entry on first Sun in the month! *3, Rue de l'Hermitage | Wed–Sat and Mon 10am–noon and 2pm–6pm, Sun 2pm–6pm*

INSIDER TIP ▶ TRENTEMOULT

Trentemoult on the southern bank of the Loire was once home to fishermen and seafarers who sailed around Cape Horn. Today, the former village is a trendy residential area with a marina and good restaurants. A shuttle boat *(navibus Loire)* goes to the Gare Maritime every 20 minutes.

FOOD & DRINK

INSIDER TIP ▶ BATEAUX NANTAIS ⚓

Eat with a view of the river! The city disappears behind you to be replaced by country homes and châteaux. Good food is also served during this 2-hour trip on the Erdre. *Quai de la Motte Rouge | tel. 02 40 14 51 14 | www.bateaux-nantais.fr | Expensive*

LA CIGALE

Traditional *brasserie* in a listed Art Nouveau building serving fish and seafood. 'The cicada' is also a wonderful choice for breakfast. *Daily | 4 Place Graslin | tel. 02 51 84 94 94 | www.lacigale.com | Moderate*

LA CIVELLE

Seafood, salads and massive steaks in an idyllic setting in Trentemoult. *Closed Sun | 21, Quai Marcel Boissard | tel. 02 40 75 46 60 | www.la-civelle.com | Moderate*

INSIDER TIP ▶ LA FRAISERAIE

Fruit ice cream to dream of, made without any additives, can be found in this parlour. *May–mid Sept daily, otherwise closed Sun/Mon | 10, Rue des Carmes | www.fraiseetsel.com*

CRÊPERIE HEB-KEN ☺

Crêpes with leek, goat's cheese or scallops flambéed in Calvados are just some of the exotic variations on the menu in this excellent *crêperie* that is packed at all times. And of course there are the sweet

LOW BUDGET

▶ If you intend visiting lots of sights in Brittany's former capital, it is worth buying the *Pass Nantes* that offers free entrance to more than 20 museums and attractions as well as unlimited use of public transport for 24 hours (20 euros), 48 hours (30 euros) or 72 hours (38 euros).

▶ If a dinner cruise or boat trip in the Loire estuary is simply too expensive, take a ● ferry across the river between Le Pellerin and Couëron for nothing *(daily | 6.30am–8.30pm)* or between Indret and Basse-Indre *(daily | 5.30am–10.30pm)* that runs every 15–20 mins.

varieties too, such as with a roast chestnut *crème*. Only local produce is used. *Closed Sun | 5–7, Rue de Guérande | tel. 02 40 48 79 83 | www.heb-ken.fr | Budget*

The *Passage Pommeraye* in Nantes has been welcoming shoppers since 1843

INSIDERTIP **LIEU-UNIQUE**
A unique atmosphere awaits you in the former LU (Lefèvre Utile) biscuit factory that has been turned into a cultural centre. Live music at weekends and a wonderful view of the château and the city can be enjoyed from the 🌿 tower. *Closed Mon evening and Sun |*

Quai Ferdinand-Favre | tel. 02 51 72 05 55 | www.lelieuunique.com | Budget

INSIDERTIP **RESTAURANT LE SQUARE**
The chef Pascal Pérou serves creative variations of timeless classic dishes in this chic restaurant near the Cité des Congrès. Try the grilled scallops in a mushroom sud or the baked *foie gras! Closed Sun | 14, Rue Jemappes | tel. 02 40 35 98 09 | www. squarenantes.com | Budget*

SHOPPING

The main shopping drag is along *Rue Crébillon* in the pedestrial precinct. The 19th century *Passage Pommeraye (Rue de la Fosse)* with its lovely wooden floors and wrought ironwork is well worth a visit. For *mascarons nantais,* a crispy chocolate pralinés, head for the *Confiserie Georges Gautier (9, Rue de la Fosse)* or *Les Rigolettes Nantaises (18, Rue de Verdun)* which is just as good. Sample the *nez grillés* made of caramel, salted butter and chocolate as well! *Talensac market (Tue-Sun | Rue de Talensac, tram 2)* sells vegetables, fish, furniture and clothes. *La Petite Boulangerie* and the ● cheese specialists *Beillevaire,* both top addresses in their respective fields, also have stands at the market. Muscadet and all the other good wines from the area can be found at the **INSIDERTIP** *Maison des Vins de Loire (15, Place du Commerce),* where it is also possible to sample them. Pretty children's clothes are available at *Million Dollar Baby (17, Rue du Château)*; presents for babies and parents at *Dröm (31, Rue de Verdun).*

SPORTS & ACTIVITIES

Electric boats for trips up the Erdre and Sèvre can be rented from *Ruban Vert (Île de Versailles | tel. 02 51 81 04 24 | www.*

rubanvert.fr). For canoe and kayak tours on the Erdre: *Contre-Courant Bivouak (Île de Versailles | tel. 06 62 28 60 48)*. Canoe tours at night on the Erdre (starting at Petit Port campsite): *Nack (Route de la Jonelière | La Chapelle-sur-Erdre | tel. 02 40 29 25 71 | www.nack.fr)*

ENTERTAINMENT

The *Opera House (1, Rue Molière | tel. 02 40 69 77 18 | www.angers-nantes-opera. com)* is well known for the high standard of its performances. A popular meeting place for the 'in' crowd is *L'Hangar à Bananes (21, Quai des Antilles | www. hangarabananes.com)* at the western end of Île de Nantes. Where bananas from Guadeloupe and Guinea were once left to ripen is now home to an art gallery, bars with views of the Loire and a nightclub.

WHERE TO STAY

HÔTEL AMIRAL ☺
This centally located hotel has been awarded the 'Clé Verte' seal of approval for meeting environmental standards. The service is friendly and the very small rooms are being renovated one by one. *49 rooms | 26, Rue Scribe | tel. 02 40 69 20 21 | www.hotel-nantes.fr | Budget*

INSIDER TIP BATEAU LE D'Ô
Sleep on the Erdre. This hotel is a boat with just one room. It has a chic galley, terrace and oodles of atmosphere. *1 room | 4, Quai Henri Barbusse | tel. 06 99 77 00 20 | www.actlieu.com | Expensive*

APPARTEMENT D'HÔTES LE LOFT
This flat in the exclusive and historical shopping arcade is a dream – not only for shop-aholics. *Passage Pommeraye | tel. 06 10 63 25 57 | www.loftnantes.com | Expensive*

POMMERAYE ☺
You can't get more central than this, located right in the pedestrian precinct. Pleasant rooms without any frills, a breakfast buffet with locally grown produce and the 'Clé Verte' environmental seal of approval all make this hotel an excellent choice. *50 rooms | 24, Rue Boileau | tel. 02 40 48 78 79 | www.hotel-pommeraye. com | Moderate*

SOZO HOTEL
The very location of this chic boutique hotel in a converted 19th-century chapel makes it unusual. The rooms are fitted with the latest high-tech equipment. *29 rooms | 16, Rue Frédéric Cailliaud | tel. 02 51 82 40 00 | www.sozohotel.fr | Expensive*

INFORMATION

9, Rue des États, and Station Prouvé (near the elephant on Île de Nantes) | tel. (*) 08 92 46 40 44 | www.nantes-tourisme. com, www.levoyageanantes.fr

PORNIC

(128 B3) *(ω B4)* ★ **The residents of this pretty little coastal town (pop. 14,000) once travelled all the way to Newfoundland to fish for cod.**

Today, there are only 15 fishing boats still used but room for 300 yachts in the marina. Romantic writers and artists such as Gustave Flaubert and Auguste Renoir were enchanted by the atmosphere here back in the 19th century. Pornic is the most important and arguably the most beautiful seaside resort on the Côte de Jade. The medieval upper town (with very few parking spaces!) is on one side of the fishing harbour with the old villa district rising up the other side and along the cliffs.

SIGHTSEEING

CHÂTEAU DE PORNIC

The oldest part of the castle dates from the 13th century. Once home to the knight Gilles de Rais, the inspiration for *Bluebeard*, it has now been divided into private flats with enviable views of the harbour.

SENTIER DES DOUANIERS ✌

This 14km (8½mi)-long 'Custom's Path' leads along the cliffs from the Corniche de Gourmalon to the Plage de la Noëveillard and offers lovely views of Noirmoutier.

FOOD & DRINK

ANNE DE BRETAGNE ✌

The head chef, Philippe Vételé, conjures up excellent culinary delights in this restaurant (and hotel) 8km (5mi) to the west in La-Plaine-sur-Mer. The food, wine and panoramic views of the sea make for an expensive but unforgettable evening *Closed Tue lunchtime and Mon as well as Sun–Tue Oct–March | Port de la Gravette | La-Plaine-sur-Mer | tel. 02 40 21 54 72 | www.annedebretagne.com | Expensive*

BEAU RIVAGE ✌

Fresh seafood right off the boat. *Closed Mon/Tue | Plage de la Birochère | tel. 02 40 82 03 08 | www.restaurant-beaurivage. com | Expensive*

L'AUBERGE LA FONTAINE AUX BRETONS

Traditional seasonal food in the hotel of the same name. *Closed Mon | Plage de la Fontaine aux Bretons | Chemin des Noëlles | tel. 02 51 74 08 08 | www.auberge la-fontaine.com | Moderate*

INSIDER TIP ▸ LA CRÊPERIE DE LA FRAISERAIE

The menu includes the widest selection of crêpes and *galettes* imaginable as well

Low tide in Pornic harbour

as ice cream specialities made with fresh fruit. Try the *galette* with scallops! *Daily | Place du Petit Nice | tel. 02 40 82 41 58 | www.lafraiseraie.com | Budget*

LA SOURCE ☃️ ☺

Excellent seafood – buffet on Wed evenings – is served in this restaurant that is also popular with locals. It forms part of the thalasso centre and enjoys sea views. The focus is on regional produce served with local wine. *Daily | Plage de la Source | tel. 02 40 82 21 21 | Moderate*

SHOPPING

● The *market (Place des Halles et de la Terrasse | Thu and Sun 9am–1pm)* is housed in a 17th-century building. An arts and crafts market is also held every Thu evening in summer. You can watch how Breton earthenware is painted by hand in the INSIDER**TIP** *Faïencerie de Pornic (Rue de la Faïencerie | www.faiencerie-pornic.fr)*.

SPORTS & BEACHES

The *Plage de la Birochère, Plage d'Étang, Plage de la Noëveillard, Plage du Portmain* and *Plage du Porteau* are all manned by lifeguards. Sports facilities range from bike and boat hire companies to diving, sailing, surfing, rowing and riding. There is also an 18-hole golf course *(Golf de Pornic | Avenue Scalby Newby | tel. 02 51 74 09 73 | www.golfdepornic.com)*.

ENTERTAINMENT

A mixed clientele gathers at the lounge bar *Key 46 (46, Quai Leray)* for cocktails, snacks and to chill out. *Les Passagers du Vent (3, Rue du Canal)* attracts chic young guests. Good cocktails are stirred and shaken in *L'Hemingway (Port de Plaisance)*. Roulette and black jack can be played in

the *casino (www.casinopornic.com)* on Quai Leray.

WHERE TO STAY

Alliance Pornic Resort Hotel & Thalasso Comfortable hotel with a thalassotherapy centre right on the seafront. *120 rooms | Plage de la Source | tel. 02 40 82 21 21 | www.thalassopornic.com | Expensive*

BEAU SOLEIL

Pleasant rooms in the best location below the castle on the harbour. *17 rooms | 70, Quai Leray | tel. 02 40 82 34 58 | www.anne debretagne.com/beausoleil | Moderate*

CHAMBRES D'HÔTES
LES VOLETS BLEUS

Charming guesthouse in a pretty garden just 200m from the harbour and 500m from the beach. *6 rooms | 22, Rue de la Source | tel. 02 40 82 65 99 | www.volets-bleus.net | Budget*

HOLIDAY FLATS

Agence Sainte-Marie | tel. 02 40 82 06 05 | www.pornic-immobilier.com

INFORMATION

Place de la Gare | tel. 02 40 82 04 40 | www.ot-pornic.fr

WHERE TO GO

SAINT-BRÉVIN-LES-PINS
(128 B2–3) (*Ø B3*)

Saint-Brévin is perfect for land yachting due to its long and particularly firm sandy beach. This small traditional seaside resort at the mouth of the Loire offers all sorts of watersports, with hiking in the *Forêt de la Pierre Attelée* and a casino. Information: *10, Rue de l'Église | tel. 02 40 27 24 32 | www.mairie-saint-brevin.fr*

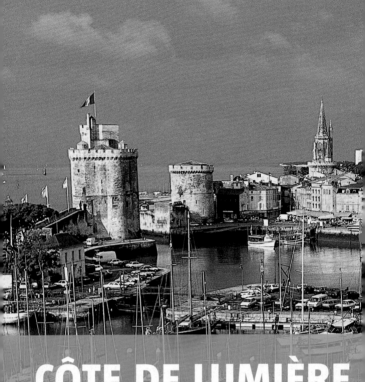

CÔTE DE LUMIÈRE

This stretch of coastline is a myriad of light. The Atlantic sparkles and glitters and a hazy shimmer hovers over the marshland in the midday heat. The countryside between Île de Noirmoutier and where the Gironde meets the sea is a wide open landscape with sheer endless expanses of sand at low tide. The smell of salt and the sound of seagulls lie in the air. This section of the coast is the perfect place for a holiday.

With well cared for, lively centres such as La Rochelle, traditional fishing villages and nature reserves as well as fashionable holiday destinations such as the little towns and villages on Ré, this is arguably the most exclusive section of the French Atlantic Coast and one that offers any amount of variety. The some 2200 hours of sunshine annually, 250km (155mi) of coast – with 140km (87mi) of sandy beaches – and unpolluted water are additional plus points. And you can buy oysters on virtually every street corner as you can buy sandwiches elsewhere. The Vendée is the most visited holiday region in France after the départements of Var and the Côte d'Azur. But, although tourism is the most important source of income virtually everywhere, agriculture and salt farming are very much part of everyday life here too.

Photo: La Rochelle

Sun, salt and sea: 2200 hours of sunshine a year and the snow-white salt ponds have given the 'Coast of Light' its name

ÎLE D'OLÉRON

(130 B3–4) *(∅ C–D8)* ★ **Oléron (pop. 21,000) is 30km (18½mi) long and 15km (9½mi) at its widest point. It still exudes its traditional charm, being a little more rustic than fashionable Ré.**

Oyter farming, brightly-coloured markets, little harbours, towering hollyhocks in cottage gardens – this is where you can relax in a rural setting. Salt marshes, two forested areas, vineyards in the north towards the cliffs on the headland and, not least of all, 100km (62mi) of cycle paths offer something for everyone. The west coast is ideal for surfers, the sheltered east coast for children and less experienced watersports enthusiasts. The 3km (2mi)-long bridge to the mainland, built in 1966,

Port des Salins on Oléron: how do they harvest salt?

is toll free. Oyster farming is the most important source of income after tourism.

WHERE TO GO ON OLÉRON

BOYARDVILLE

This pretty village on the east coast has a fishing port and marina, good shops and restaurants and a vast sandy beach. *Fort Boyard* was built offshore by Napoleon in the 19th century on an outcrop of rock and sand to defend the mouth of the Charente. It sits in the water like an oval pebble and can be viewed from the outside only – boat trips available from Boyardville. The wooded area, the *Forêt des Saumonards*, starts to the north of the village.

LE CHÂTEAU-D'OLÉRON

The first village you come to on the island is so delightful that you might not want to go any further! The largest *market* on the island (food, clothes and crafts) takes place on Sun *(9am–1pm)* on the *Place de la République*. The ⚲ *citadelle* offers lovely views of the mainland. **INSIDER TIP**

Artists' studios occupy the 18 little brightly-coloured wooden huts in the fishing port below. These were previously used for oyster farming until EU legislation forced them to move into 'proper' buildings. Now you can watch painters and potters at work and of course buy their wares.

INSIDER TIP *Jardins Aliénor (4 rooms | 11, Rue de Maréchal Foch | tel. 05 46 76 48 30 | www.lesjardinsdalienor.com | Expensive)* is a comfortable and beautifully furnished hotel with a very good restaurant. Information: *Place de la République | tel. 05 46 47 60 51 | www.ot-chateauoleron.fr*

LA COTINIÈRE

250 fishermen still go about their business here making La Cotinière less a picturesque harbour and more a bustling fishing port. Fish for dinner can be bought in the *Marché de Victorine* right on the harbour. The restaurant ⚲ *L'Écailler (daily | 65, Rue du Port | tel. 05 46 47 10 31 | www.ecailler-oleron.com | Moderate)* serves delicious seafood with a view of the harbour. You can also eat in *La Marine* bar which is

where the party crowd meet until all hours of the night.

LE GRAND-VILLAGE-PLAGE

The place gets its name from the 15km (9½mi)-long beach – a paradise for sun-worshippers and watersports enthusiasts. In Le Petit Village there is a salt harbour and the *Écomusée du Port-des-Salines (April/May Tue–Sat 9.30am–noon and 2pm–6.30pm, Sun/Mon 2pm–6.30pm, June and Sept Tue–Sat 10am–noon and 2pm–6pm, Sun/Mon 2pm–6pm, July/Aug Mon–Sat 10am–7pm, Sun 2pm–7pm)*, that gives an insight into the secrets of salt and oyster farming. There are also boats for hire and a market where oysters can be sampled. The restaurant ● *Le Relais des Salines (daily | Port des Salines | tel. 05 46 75 82 42 | www.lerelaisdessalines.com | Moderate)*, located in a row of little oyster farm huts, is famous for its seafood. Information: *Boulevard de la Plage | tel. 05 46 47 58 00 | www.legrandvillageplage.fr*

SAINT-DÉNIS-D'OLÉRON

The most northerly village on the island (pop. 1200) has a large marina, a *church* with a Romanesque portal and a 14th-century tower. The 46m (150ft)-high lighthouse, the *Phare de Chassiron (July/Aug daily 10am–8pm, otherwise 10am–12.15pm and 2pm–5pm)* at Oléron's most northerly Pointe de Chassiron, is also well worth visiting. Information: *Boulevard d'Antioche | tel. 05 46 47 95 53 | www.st-denis-oleron.com*

SAINT-GEORGES-D'OLÉRON

The largest village on the island (pop. 3350) is in the north near a 15km (5mi)-long beach with lots of campsites. To the south, its adjoins the *Forêt Domaniale de Domino*. At the centre of the village is the Romanesque *church* (11th/12th century) with a richly decorated façade. In summer,

the *market hall* dating from the 19th century is a popular meeting place.

The pleasant *Hotel L'Hermitage (34 rooms | 198, Route de l'Hermitage | tel. 05 46 76 52 56 | www.lhermitage-oleron.com | Budget)* is 800m from the beach Les Sables Vignier. It boasts a heated outdoor pool, restaurant and friendly service. The campsite *La Caravane Oléronaise | tel. 05 46 76 52 31 | www.campingsablesvignier plage.com* can be recommended. It has

MARCO POLO HIGHLIGHTS

⭐ **Île d'Oléron**
Time to unwind by cycling or hiking, or over a plate of freshly caught seafood on the harbour in La Cotinière → p. 47

⭐ **Île de Ré**
The most glamourous of the islands on the Atlantic coast → p. 50

⭐ **Grand Marché in La Rochelle**
On Wed and Sat the market spreads over the whole district – wonderful to look at and for shopping → p. 56

⭐ **The Old Town in La Rochelle**
Café hopping on the harbour → p. 53

⭐ **Île de Noirmoutier**
Buy salt where it is harvested, cycle through scented pine woods, stroll around the main centre in the evening – and, of course, soak up the sun on the beach → p. 58

⭐ **Marais Poitevin**
Wonderful boat trips through the green labyrinth of canals → p. 60

33 pitches, a restaurant and pool and is also close to Les Sables Vigniers. Information: *28, Rue des Dames | tel. 05 46 76 63 75 | www.saint-georges-oleron.com*

SAINT-PIERRE-D'OLÉRON

The capital of the island (pop. 6000) is surrounded by supermarkets but has a pretty town centre with lots of shops and places to go. A market is held on the last Tue of every month on the huge *Place Gambetta* which otherwise doubles as a free car park. Concerts from blues to salsa are held here in the summer, as is an evening market for local products. The interactive *Musée de l'Île d'Oléron (April–June and Sept/Oct daily 10am–noon and 2pm–6pm, July/Aug 10am–7pm, Nov–March Tue–Sun 2pm–6pm)* that documents the island's history is also on this square. A roofed market operates every day in summer and during the school holidays, as well as on Tue, Thu, Sat and Sun in the low season, on Place Camille Mémain.

The 17th-century *church* with its light-coloured, 43m (147ft)-high tower that used to help ships navigate, and the *Lanterne des Morts* – the 'Lantern of the Dead' – a 23.5m (77ft)-high tower from the 12th century, are among the sights worth seeing. There is also a *botanical garden (La Boirie | April–Oct Mon–Sat 10am–noon and 3pm–7pm, Sun 3pm–7pm | www.lesjardinsdelaboirie.com)* with plants from all over the world. *La Maison des Aïeules (13, Rue Pierre Loti | tours June–Sept Thu 10.15am starting at the Office de Tourisme)* was the home of the novelist Pierre Loti (1850–1923). He spent his holidays here as a child with his parents; later the house was a source of inspiration. He is buried in the grounds.

The 9-hole *golf course (Vieille Perrotine | tel. 05 46 47 11 59)* is to the north of the town. The young visitors who crowd

INSIDER TIP ★ Café *Le Bus Stop (Rue d'Aliénor*

d'Aquitaine) sprawl out onto the road in the evening. Information: *Place Gambetta | tel. 05 46 47 11 39 | www.saint-pierre-oleron-tourisme.fr*

ÎLE DE RÉ

(130 A–B2) *(Ø C–D7)* ★ The toll to cross the almost 3km (1¾mi)-long bridge to the Île de Ré (pop. 17,000) costs 16 euros during the high season. Not very welcoming – but it's not supposed to be either. Ever since the bridge was completed in 1988, the islanders have been torn between the luxury of being able to drive to La Rochelle in less than 20 minutes and the fear that their island could be inundated by many too many day-trippers. It was discussed at length as to whether to abolish the toll or not and just keep the environmental charge of a little more than 3 euros. However, the fear of too many visitors finally won the day. The toll may well be called an *écotaxe* rather than *péage* but, at 16 euros, it is only 50 cents cheaper than before. In the low season, the toll has been lowered from 9 to 8 euros. It is still a much discussed topic on the island. Île de Ré has 110km (68mi) of cycle paths – often idyllic stretches away from any roads; bikes can be hired in every village – long sandy beaches and expensive resorts. Everything one could wish for an active but not exactly cheap beach holiday can be found here.

On the north coast there are a number of villages and harbours and an almost 15km (9mi)-long beach down the Atlantic coast. The most beautiful beaches are *Plage de la Conche* and *Plage du Marchais* in the northwest corner. Surfing is one of the most popular pastimes on the island. There are more than enough opportunities to either watch others falling into the water or to risk going out on a board yourself. The surfing hotspots are *Lizay* beach near Les-Portes-en-Ré, *La Pergola* in La-Couarde-sur-Mer, the south beach in *Rivedoux-Plage*, *Les Grenettes* and *Pas des Biettes* in Sainte Marie and *Gros Jonc* in Le-Bois-Plage.

Île de Ré, however, also has a traditional side. As in Guérande and on Noirmoutier and Oléron, salt is also harvested on Ré. The island's countryside is largely unspoilt. More than 300 types of bird have been counted in the sanctuary near Ars.

WHERE TO GO ON RÉ

ARS-EN-RÉ

The prominent black-and-white church tower in this village (pop. 1300) can be seen from a long way away, rising above the salt marshes like a navigation mark for ships – which in fact is what it really is used for. Well-kept narrow streets lead to a selection of good shops and restaurants. The **INSIDER TIP** *Café du Commerce (daily | 6, Quai Prée | tel. 05 46 29 41 57 | www. cafcom-ars.com | Budget)* on the harbour – the most important marina on the island – is well worth a visit. It is decorated with souvenirs from all over the world, from masks to golfclubs and engravings of old ships. The elegant but uncluttered atmosphere and excellent regional specialities – fish and seafood as well as potatoes from the island – make *Ô de Mer Bistrot Gourmand (closed Mon | 5, Rue Thiers | tel. 05 46 29 23 33 | www.odemerbistrotgourmand. fr | Moderate)* a good choice. The hotel *Thalacap (89 rooms | Avenue d'Antioche | tel. 05 46 29 10 00 | www.thalacap.com | Expensive)* has its own thalassotherapy centre. Information: *26, Place Carnot | tel. 05 46 29 46 09 | www.iledere-arsenre.com*

LE-BOIS-PLAGE-EN-RÉ

This almost 15km (9mi)-long beach in the south of the island is a real holiday para-

Très chic but not over-the-top: the marina on Ré

dise. To the west is the pretty village *La Couarde-sur-Mer,* followed by *Bois,* with Sainte-Marie-de-Ré to the southeast. Le Bois-Plage, the largest settlement on the south coast, is surrounded by woods and vineyards. Ré grapes are made into wine, Cognac and Pineau. The beach is particularly suitable for children as there are no sudden drops. You can swim regardless of the tides. Several companies rent out catamarans, surfboards and kayaks and give sailing lessons, e.g. *École de Voile du Bois-Plage La Cabane Verte (tel. 05 46 09 94 73 | www.lacabaneverte.com)* on the Plage de Gros Jonc; surfing and windsurfing at *Ré Surf (Plage de Gros Jonc | tel. 06 30 08 12 81 | www.re-surf.com)*.

The hotel *Les Gollandières (32 rooms | Avenue Les Gollandières | tel. 05 46 09 23 99 | www.lesgollandieres.com | Expensive)*, with a pool and restaurant, is situated just behind the dunes on *Plage des Gollandières*. The hotel and holiday apartment complex *Jerodel (12 rooms | 35, Rue de la Glacière | tel. 05 46 09 96 42 | www.jerodel.com | Expensive)* has a heated pool and is just a short distance out of the village but also close to the beach. The hotel *L'Océan (30 rooms | 172, Rue Saint-Martin | tel. 05 46 09 23 07 | www.re-hotel-ocean.com | Moderate)* is stylishly but unostentatiously furnished.

It boasts a pool, a spa, a lovely garden and a restaurant. Information: *Rue des Barjottes | tel. 05 46 09 23 26 | www.lebois plageenre-tourisme.com*

LA FLOTTE

An idyllic holiday resort with up-market shops and restaurants around a pretty harbour. Boutiques and hairdressers jostle for space on the Rue Général-de-Gaulle. A market is held every morning in summer on the Place de Marché. Fish specialities at the restaurant ✺ *L'Écailler (closed Mon | 3, Quai de Sénac | tel. 05 46 09 56 40 | www.lecailler-iledere.com | Expensive)* can be enjoyed with a lovely view of the harbour. The elegant *Hotel Richelieu (40 rooms | 44, Avenue de la Plage | tel. 05 46 09 60 70 | www.hotel-lerichelieu.com | Expensive)* on the beach has its own thalassotherapy centre. *Le Français (33 rooms | 1, Cours Félix Faure | tel. 05 46 09 60 06 | www.hotellefrancais.*

Square white houses, umbrella pines and street cafés: the promenade in La Flotte

com | *Budget)*, located on the harbour with its own restaurant, is more down-to-earth. Information: *Quai de Sénac | tel. 05 46 09 60 38 | www.ot-laflotte.fr*

SAINT-MARTIN-DE-RÉ

The island's glamourous little capital (pop. 2600), with its marina, chic bars and restaurants and elegant hotels, is like Saint-Tropez's twin town on the Atlantic. This is the liveliest place on the island, especially in the evening. The town is encircled by ramparts that have been declared a Unesco World Heritiage Site. Cars must be parked outside (free of charge). The 🔊 *church tower* offers lovely views of the town. Choose a seat at one of the cafés and watch the comings and goings on the streets and in the harbour that drains completely at low tide.

While strolling around the picturesque harbour, a visit to the ice cream parlour INSIDER TIP *La Martinière* is well worth

while: try the caramel or *fleur de sel* ice cream. Fish and seafood are to be found in *Le Belem (daily | 17, Quai de la Poitevinière | tel. 05 46 09 20 99 | la-martiniere. fr | Moderate)* and regional cuisine in *Le Bistrot du Marin (closed Thu | 10, Quai Nicolas Baudin | tel. 05 46 68 74 66 | www. bistrotdumarin.fr | Moderate)* on the island in the harbour. The dignified and elegant *Hôtel de Toiras* on the old harbour *(20 rooms | 1, Quai Job Foran | tel. 05 46 35 40 32 | www.hotel-de-toiras.com | Expensive)* has a 17th-century façade and a pretty garden. The hotel *Les Colonnes (30 rooms | 19, Quai Job Foran | tel. 05 46 09 21 58 | www.hotellescolonnes. com | Moderate)* with lovely 🔊 rooms, some of which have delightful views of the sea, lies in the middle of the island in the harbour. The organisation *Pierre et Vacances (Rue des Gouverneurs | www. pierreetvacances.com)* has holiday flats in club-like complexes. Information: *2, Quai Nicolas Baudin | tel. 05 46 09 20 06 | www. saint-martin-de-re.net*

LA ROCHELLE

◾◾◾ **MAP INSIDE BACK COVER**
◾◾◾ **(130 B2–3)** *(𝄞 D7)* **La Rochelle (pop. 80,000) is a city in miniature which boasts an international film festival, the 'Francofolies' music festival in July and France's most recently founded university.**

Les Minimes marina is the largest on the Atlantic coast in Europe and gives La Rochelle its southern flair. La Pallice harbour is to the west of the town where the Germans constructed two submarine bunkers in World War II. Today, boats are built and fitted out here. The picturesque ⭐ *Old Town* behind the Old Port and a row of buildings fronted by cafés, conceals a mass of shops and restaurants and has a relaxed, bustling atmosphere. The arcades that stretch for almost 3km (1¾mi) make shopping in the rain a pleasure. But make sure you look up too – lots of the façades are decorated with gargoyles and carved stone heads.

Just like Nantes and Bordeaux, the town benefitted from trade between Europe, West Africa and the Caribbean. The vineyards and salt ponds also contributed to its wealth, as did the port of course. This remained unchanged until the Siege of La Rochelle during the Wars of Religion in the 17th century when the town was a Protestant stronghold. After 13 months, only 5400 of the 28,000 inhabitants were still alive; the town was stripped of all its privileges and rights and it was to be 300 years before it would flourish again as it had done before.

La Rochelle is easy to explore by bike – not only thanks to the many cycle paths but also to the 😊 INSIDER TIP yellow bikes which can be rented on Place de Verdun and at the Office de Tourisme on the Old Port. After paying a deposit, they cost 1 euro an hour after the third hour. The road surfaces may not always be ideal but they have a lot of stories to tell. The bumpy cobbles in the shipowners' district around Rue Nicolas Venette come from the Saint Lawrence River in Canada – a reminder of trading times with Quebec, a city that was founded by a native of La Rochelle in 1608.

La Rochelle has a state-of-the-art 'green' political strategy not only reflected in the free yellow bikes. It also has a modern transport concept that includes the 😊 *Libre Service Véhicule Électrique (www. larochelle.comox.fr)* available for a small fee at seven electric charging stations.

SIGHTSEEING

AQUARIUM ●

10,000 different species and 20 types of shark that swim over visitors' heads as well as a piranha basin in the Amazon hothouse. The undersea world here is fascinating. *Bassin des Grands Yachts | April–Sept daily 9–8pm (July/Aug 9am–11pm), Oct–March 10am–8pm | www. aquarium-larochelle.com*

ÉGLISE SAINT-SAUVEUR

The to-ings and fro-ings of the Wars of Religion can be traced in this church on the harbour. The tower dates from the 15th century, the nave was rebuilt in the 17th century after the Catholics were expelled in the 16th century and all Catholic churches in La Rochelle were demolished. The stones were used for the town's fortifications. Only the church towers were left – as watchtowers and platforms for canons. After the Counter Reformation everything changed once again; today, there are only a few Protestant churches here.

HÔTEL DE VILLE

The Town Hall has been the mayor's office for 700 years. It looks like a little knight's castle with its fortified towers and crenel-

---

CITY **WHERE TO START?**

The **Vieux Port** is the place to start any visit. From here, the most important sights in the Old Town and port can all be reached easily on foot or on one of the yellow rental bikes. A lovely way to reach the town centre is on a *bus de mer* from the free car park Les Minimes. The car parks Bernard Loitessier at the Musée Maritime, Rieupeyrot next to the Technoforum and the Esplanade de Parcs in the centre are also free. For those arriving by train, lines 41 and 43 go to Place du Verdun.

There are 20 different species of shark alone in the aquarium in La Rochelle

lations. It looks out across the Place de l'Hôtel de Ville to the cafés La Poste and La Renaissance. The inner courtyard is open to the public *(guided tours July/Aug daily 3pm and 4pm, June and Sept 3pm, Oct–May Sat/Sun 3pm).*

MUSÉE DES BEAUX ARTS

European painting from the 15th–20th centuries in a Neo-Classicist *palais. 28, Rue Gargoulleau | July–Sept Mon and Wed–Fri 10am–12.30pm and 1.45pm–6pm, Sat/ Sun 2pm–6pm, Oct–June Mon and Wed–Fri 9.30am–12.30pm and 1.45pm–5pm, Sat/Sun 2pm–6pm*

MUSÉE DU FLACON À PARFUM

This small museum has a collection of more than 1000 unusual perfume bottles and powder boxes. *33, Rue du Temple | July/Aug Mon–Sat 10.30am–7pm, Sept– June Tue–Sat 2.30pm–7pm*

MUSÉE MARITIME

The everyday life of meteorologists and fishermen at sea is brought to life on the weather ship 'France I' and a steam-operated fishing vessel. The **INSIDER TIP** charming *Bar du France I*, that is also open in the evenings, can be found on France I. *Bassin des Chalutiers | April–Sept daily 10am–6.30pm (July/Aug 7pm) | www.museemaritimelarochelle.fr*

MUSÉE DU NOUVEAU MONDE

In La Rochelle, the New World generally means Canada. The exhibition in a magnificent patrician's house traces the links between France and America with colonial furniture, paintings, documents, etc. *10, Rue Fleuriau | July–Sept Mon and Wed–Fri 10am–12.30pm and 1.45pm– 6pm, Sat/Sun 2pm–6pm, Oct–June Mon and Wed–Fri 9.30am–12.30pm and 1.45pm–5pm, Sat/Sun 2pm–6pm*

LA ROCHELLE

TOWERS ☼

The 14th-century *Tour de la Chaîne* and *Tour Saint-Nicolas* once guarded the port and testify to the wealth and extent of the town that had to be defended. The 70m (230ft)-high *Tour de la Lanterne* was once a lighthouse and a prision for a time, as testified by the graffiti. *April–Sept daily*

sels and fish. The writer Georges Simenon was a regular guest here. *Daily | 54, Rue Chaudrier | tel. 05 46 41 39 79 | Budget*

RICHARD & CHRISTOPHER COUTANCEAU ☼

Richard Coutanceau's cuisine has been awarded 2 Michelin stars without a break

Imposing towers guard the entrance to the Vieux Port in La Rochelle

10am–6.30pm, Oct–March 10am–1pm and 2.30pm–5.30pm

FOOD & DRINK

ANDRÉ

Fish and seafood at the foot of the two towers on the Old Port. *Daily | 5, Rue Saint-Jean du Pérot | tel. 05 46 41 28 24 | www.barandre.com | Moderate*

CAFÉ DE LA PAIX

Beautiful Art Nouveau café with a very varied menu ranging from salads to mus-

since 1986. The excellent food is topped by a truly heavenly view of the sea. *Closed Sun | Plage de la Concurrence | tel. 05 46 41 48 19 | Expensive*

SHOPPING

Rue des Merciers, Rue du Palais and *Rue Chaudrier* are good addresses for clothes, accessories and culinary souvenirs – for which the *market hall (daily | Place du Marché)* is well worth a visit. The ★ *Grand Marché* is held on Wed and Sat. The market is so big that the whole of the surrounding area, the *Quartier du Marché,* is also full of flower, cheese and fruit stands too. Regional specialities such as Cognac, Pineau des Charentes and the *tourteau fromager* cheese pastry can also be found here. A great place to visit, to go shopping and take pictures!

SPORTS & ACTIVITIES

Sailing *(École de Voile Rochelaise | Avenue de la Capitainerie | tel. 05 46 44 49 20 | www.voile-rochelaise.com)* and boating *(Aunis Motonautic | Les Minimes | tel. 05 46 44 23 66 | www.aunismotonautic.fr)* are all part of any maritime experience.

ENTERTAINMENT

The nicest way to spend an evening is to drift from one café to the next around the harbour. Later on you can head for the clubs *L'Oxford (Plage de la Concurrence | www.oxford-club.fr)* and *Le Triolet (8, Rue des Carmes | letrioletclub.com).*

WHERE TO STAY

BEST WESTERN CHAMPLAIN FRANCE ANGLETERRE

Grand villa right next to Place de Verdun with a large garden for breakfast and to relax in, and very spacious rooms. *36 rooms | 30, Rue Rambaud | tel. 05 46 41 23 99 | www.hotelchamplain.com | Moderate*

RÉSIDENCE DE FRANCE

The best hotel in townhas every creature comfort including a heated outdoor pool and an underground car park. There are also some flats with the same hotel service for between 2–4 people in an adjoining building. *16 rooms | 43, Rue du Minage | tel. 05 46 28 06 00 | www.hotel-larochelle.com | Expensive*

COMFORT HOTEL SAINT NICOLAS

Pleasant hotel on a small square near the fishing port. *86 rooms | 13, Rue Sardinerie | tel. 05 46 41 71 55 | www.hotel-saint-nicolas.com | Moderate*

INFORMATION

2, Quai Georges Simenon | tel. 05 46 41 14 68 | www.larochelle-tourisme.com

WHERE TO GO

CHÂTELAILLON-PLAGE (130 B–C3) *(🕮 D7)*

This seaside resort (pop. 5500) is 12km (7½mi) to the south on a 3km (2mi)-long fine sandy beach where wind and kite-surfers congregate at high tide. The villas dating from the Belle Époque and the promenade lined with tamarisk trees with a view of the islands Aix and Oléron, are real plus points. There is also a casino with an adjoining nightclub. Information: *5, Avenue de Strasbourg | tel. 05 46 56 26 97 | www.chatelaillon-plage-tourisme.fr*

ÎLE D'AIX (130 B3) *(🕮 D8)*

20km (12½mi) to the south of La Rochelle is the ferry port Fouras. In just 30 mins. by boat from here you can reach the traffic-free Île d'Aix (pop. 200). A village enclosed within the walls of the Fort de la Rade awaits visitors, surrounded by a natural paradise – the perfect backdrop for a quiet day by the sea or an extended exploration of the island on a rented bike *(Cyclaix | tel. 05 46 84 58 23 | www.cyclaix.com).* The *Musée Napoléonien (April–Sept daily, Oct–March Wed–Mon 9.30am–noon and 2pm–5pm, Oct 6pm | www.musees-nationaux-napoleoniens.org)* traces the final three days Bonaparte spent on French soil in July 1815 on Aix, before being exiled to St Helena. His death mask, several letters – including his unsuccessful appeal for asylum in England – as well as his bedroom are on show. In the affiliated *Musée Afrique* opposite, a stuffed camel that Napoleon supposedly rode during his campaign in Egypt can be seen as well as a variety of big game and African works of art. Information: *6, Rue Gourgaud | tel. 05 46 83 01 82 | www.iledaix.fr*

use this *Passage du Gois*, several cars having been washed away by the incoming tide in the past.

Parts of Noirmoutier which is an ● ideal place for cycling (rental bikes available in every village) are actually below sea level. Long sandy beaches open up beyond dense pine forests. *Plage de Luzéronde* on

Hollyhocks grow in many places on the Côte de Lumière such as here on Île de Noirmoutier

ÎLE DE NOIRMOUTIER ★
(128 A–B4) (*⑰ A–B4*)

Salt ponds, oyster beds, fishing harbours, sailing boats and white houses adorned with flowering hibiscus characterise this island (pop. 10,000) that is a good 20km (12½mi) long. The island can be reached via a toll-free bridge (180km/112mi from La Rochelle and 70km/43mi from Nantes), by ferry from Pornic (only in July/August) or across a 4km (2½mi)-long paved causeway that can be crossed at low tide and disappears at high tide when only the tips of the traffic signs can be seen sticking out of the water. Tourists seldom

the western coast is a nudist beach. Sailing schools and watersports centres are dotted all over the island.

The main centre, *Noirmoutier-en-l'Île*, with its shops, restaurants, Romanesque and Gothic *Saint-Philbert* church and its well-preserved 12th-century castle, is the attractive focal point of island life. The *Musée du Château (Place d'Armes | mid June–mid Sept daily 10am–7pm, mid Sept–mid Nov and mid May–mid June Wed–Mon 1pm–6pm, Feb–mid April Wed–Mon 2pm–6pm, mid April–mid May daily 11am–6pm)*, housed in the castle, traces the island's history. The ● *Musée des Traditions de l'Île*

(Place de l'Église | July/Aug daily 10am–12.30pm and 3pm–7pm, April–June and Sept–mid Oct daily 3pm–6pm) explains everything about fishing and salt farming, whereas the *Musée de la Construction Navale* (Rue de l'Écluse | expected to reopen after renovation in 2013) focuses on everything to do with shipbuilding.

The small elegant hotel INSIDER TIP ▶ *Blanc Marine* (5 rooms | 1, Rue de l'Acquenette | tel. 02 51 39 99 11 | www.blanc-marine.net | *Moderate–Expensive*) is lovingly managed by Véronique and Jean Dalric who give it a very personal touch. It has a pool and a delightful garden. A very opulent breakfast – by French standards – is included in the price. *Hôtel du Bois de la Chaize* (8 rooms | 23, Avenue de la Victoire | tel. 02 51 39 04 62 | www.hotel-noirmoutier.com | *Budget–Moderate*) is a charming small hotel between Plage des Dames and the harbour and is especially suitable for families as it has rooms sleeping 4–5. Imaginative interpretations of traditional island dishes can be found in the small restaurant *Le Vélo Noir* (closed Sun/Mon, Wed in July/Aug | 13, Rue du Vieil Hôpital | tel. 02 51 35 85 29 | www.levelonoir.fr | *Moderate*). The trendy crowd gathers at *Café Noir* (4, Quai Cassard | tel. 02 51 39 00 75). Noirmoutier-en-l'Île is 2km (1¼mi) from the sea. To the south is a nature reserve with salt marshes and bird nesting sites.

The chic *Plage des Dames* that stretches beyond the *Bois de la Chaize* across several bays is where there are a number of villas owned by politicians and celebrities. To the north is the lovely fishing village and holiday resort *L'Herbaudière*. Alexandre Couillon conjures up creative fish dishes in his 1-Michelin-Star restaurant INSIDER TIP ▶ *La Marine* (closed Wed | 5, Rue Marie Lemonnier | tel. 02 51 39 23 09 | *Moderate*). Fish and seafood from the waters around Noirmoutier dominate the menu at the lovely restaurant INSIDER TIP ▶ *La Plage de Jules* (daily | Plage des Dames/30, Avenue Georges Clemenceau | tel. 02 51 39 06 87 | www.laplagedejules.com | *Budget*), but steak lovers find what their hearts desire here too. Breakfast and cocktails are also available. The villages of *La Bosse*, *L'Épine* and *Barbâtre* with their narrow alleyways, low white houses and flowering hibiscus are also extremely picturesque. Information: *Route du Pont | tel. 02 51 39 80 71 | www.ile-noirmoutier.com*

ÎLE D'YEU (128 A5) (*∅ A5*)

Sandy beaches to the east, the wild Côte Sauvage to the southwest and pine and oak forests make up the Île d'Yeu (pop. 5000). Located 20km (12½mi) from the mainland, it covers an area of 9mi². It can be reached by ferry from Fromentine and Saint-Gilles-Croix-de-Vie (www.compagnie-yeu-continent.fr, www.compagnie vendeenne.com).

Pretty *Port-Joinville* on the sheltered east coast is the main settlement on the island. The principle beach is in neighbouring *Ker-Chalon* with another lovely beach in *Plage des Sabias*. Yeu is best explored by bike (available from dozens of rental places) especially as many of the sheltered beaches can only be reached on foot or by bike. The ruins of the *Vieux-Château* on the Côte Sauvage and the natural harbour *Port-de-la-Meule* are both well worth visiting. Dolmens and menhirs testify to the island's early settlement. The most famous is the *Dolmen de la Planche à Puare* on the northwest coast. The stone formation is estimated to be 5000 years old.

The hotel *Grand Large* (22 rooms | 1, Rue du Courseau | tel. 02 51 58 36 77 | www.hotel-legrandlarge.fr | *Budget*) is right on the harbour in Port-Joinville. Two charming *chambres d'hôtes* 50m and 500m respectively from the sea are run by M. et Mme. Groisard (49, Rue Saint-Hilaire | La

Citadelle | tel. 02 51 58 42 30 | Budget; 11, Rue Pierre Henry | Port-Joinville | tel. 02 51 58 55 24 | www.yeu-sejour.com | Budget). Information: *1, Rue du Marché | tel. 02 51 58 32 58 | www.ile-yeu.fr*

MARAIS POITEVIN ★ ●
(130 B–C 1–2) *(🕮 D–E 6–7)*

This extensive marshland area *(www.marais-poitevin.com)* lies 30km (19mi) to the northeast of La Rochelle. It is criss-crossed by thousands of canals. Since time immemorial, the people here have used flat, black boats as a means of transport – whether it is to go to church or the baker's. Tourists today can do just the same – with a guide, as the network of waterways is one huge labyrinth for the uninitiated. But what a beautiful one! Poplars, willows, ash and tall reeds line the banks watched over by herons. You may even catch a glimpse of a beaver. Starting points include *Arçais, Coulon, Damvix* and *Maillezais.*

An exceptional place to stay which has been ecologically planned down to the last detail is INSIDER TIP *Les Gîtes des Six Moulins (22, Rue des Six Moulins | tel. 06 32 39 34 22 | www.gitesdes6moulins.com | Expensive)* in *Vix.* The pool is fed by pure filtered rainwater, free of any chemicals, the buildings were constructed personally by the owner ensuring that as few resources as possible were used and the building materials were all sourced locally. The houses each accommodate up to 6 people and have their own terraces and barbecue areas.

NOTRE-DAME-DE-MONTS
(128 B4) *(🕮 B5)*

This seaside resort (pop. 1500) some 150km (68mi) north of La Rochelle provides perfect conditions for watersports and kayak tours on the marshland canals *(Pôle Nautique | 20, Boulevard des Dunes | tel. 02 51 58 05 66). Le Jardin du Vent* (see 'Travel with Kids') and the open-air museum *La Maison de la Dune et de la Fôret (50, Avenue Abbé Thibaud | July/Aug Mon–Fri 10am–12.30pm and 3pm–6.30pm, April–June and Sept Wed 2.30pm–6pm),* which focuses on the farming traditions of the Vendée, are both very interesting. A superb view over the marshlands and across to Noirmoutier can be enjoyed from the 70m (230ft)-high INSIDER TIP *Salle Panoramique (July/Aug Sun–Fri 10am–7.30pm, Sat 2pm–7.30pm, May/June and Sept Wed–Sun 2pm–6.30pm, Oct/Nov 2pm–6pm | www.kulmino.fr)* in the water tower. Information: *6, Rue de la Barre | tel. 02 51 58 84 97 | www.notre-dame-de-monts.fr*

ROCHEFORT (130 C3) *(🕮 D8)*

A major attraction in Rochefort (pop. 26,000), some 30km (19mi) to the south, is the *Corderie Royale,* the royal rope factory, a 375m-long, Baroque building with a landscaped garden situated on the river bank. It comprises the *Centre International de la Mer (July/Aug daily 9am–7pm, April–June and Sept 10am–7pm, Feb/March and Oct–Dec 10am–12.30pm and 2pm–6pm | www.corderie-royale.com)* with an exhibition on the former royal rope manufacture. A reproduction of the *historical three-master, Hermione,* is moored along the bank *(July/Aug daily 9am–7pm, April–June and Sept 10am–7pm, Oct–March 10am–12.30pm and 2pm–6pm).* Information: *Avenue Sadi-Carnot | tel. 05 46 99 08 60 | www.ville-rochefort.fr, www.paysrochefortais-tourisme.com, www.rochefort-ocean.com*

LES SABLES-D'OLONNE
(128 C6) *(🕮 B–C6)*

This lively resort (pop. 16,000), with its 3km (2mi)-long beach promenade *Le Remblai,* is 80km (50mi) to the northwest of La

Rochelle. The *fishing port*, the 11th-century chapel *Prieuré Saint-Nicolas* and the ☝ *Tour d'Arundel* lighthouse at the entrance to the harbour channel are well worth seeing.

ists can leave their swimming things are a feature of the long beach that grows considerably at low tide. If you want even more room to yourselves, head for *Grande Plage* further to the right which stretches

Endless sandy beaches and a continuous cool breeze: Les Sables-d'Olonne

Delicious seafood can be found at *Le Clipper (closed Tue/Wed | 19 bis, Quai Guiné | tel. 02 51 32 03 61 | Moderate)* on the harbour. Just 50m from the Grande Plage is the comfortable hotel *Arc en Ciel (37 rooms | 13, Rue Chanzy | tel. 02 51 96 92 50 | www.arcencielhotel.com | Budget– Moderate)*. Information: *1, Promenade Joffre | tel. 02 51 96 85 85 | www.ot-lessables dolonne.fr*

SAINT-GILLES-CROIX-DE-VIE
(128 B5) (*ⓜ B5*)
Saint-Gilles-Croix-de-Vie (pop. 7000) is a friendly resort ideal for families a good 100km (62mi) north of La Rochelle. 250 sardine fishermen still operate from here. The little blue wooden cabins where tour-

along a strip of land between the sea and the mouth of the river Vie. It can only be reached on foot, by bike or water bus (departing from the fishing port).

A INSIDERTIP *craft market* is held every evening in July and August on Place du Vieux Port. A choice of INSIDERTIP ▶ 42 different mussel dishes can be found at *Moulerie de la Gare (closed Mon Sept– May | 52, Quai de la République | tel. 02 51 55 07 28 | Budget)*. Information: *Place de la Gare | tel. 02 51 55 03 66 | www. stgillescroixdevie.com*

The coast around neighbouring *Saint-Hilaire-de-Riez* is steeper and more rugged. Further north is *Saint-Jean-de-Monts*, famous for its wide sandy beach but lined by hotel complexes and blocks of flats.

LA TRANCHE-SUR-MER
(128 B2) (*₥ C6*)

13km (8mi) of fine sandy beach and some 250 days of sunshine a year have turned this village (pop. 2100) with its white-washed cottages, 40km (25mi) north of La Rochelle, into a miniature paradise for sun-worshippers and watersports enthu-siasts. Families with children will find any amount of things to do here too. Information: *Place de la Liberté | tel. 02 51 30 33 96 | www.ot-latranchesurmer.fr*

ROYAN

(130 C5) (*₥ D9*) **The roofed market looks like a huge umbrella and its bustling promenade, packed with bars, boutiques and restaurants, curves around the marina like two outstretched arms.**

This town (pop. 19,000), located on the northern bank of the Gironde estuary around a 2km (1¼mi)-wide bay, has little in common with other resorts in the area apart from its long beach. In the 19th and early 20th century, the moneyed from Bordeaux and writers and artists came here. Émile Zola took photos of the coast and Picasso painted the Café des Bains. That nothing remains of the old town of Royan except for pictures and memories is due to the German army which resisted the heavy attacks of the Allied Forces in January 1945. 85% of the town was destroyed.

Opinions were divided about how the town should be rebuilt after the war – true to the original or something completely new and different. An urban planner had seen buildings designed by the German-Brazilian architect Oscar Niemeyer and the result has a hint of of the tropical.

SIGHTSEEING

ÉGLISE NOTRE-DAME
The church, built in the 1950s out of re-inforced concrete, looks like an organ. The height of the nave varies accordingly from 28–36m (92–118ft). It is just one building inspired by the architecture of Brazil that redefined Royan after being bombed in the war.

FRONT DE MER
A seemingly endless, three-storey com-plex of restaurants and shops stretches around the bay in a wide curve. When it was built, the expansive façade fronting the sea was considered the epitome of modern urban planning.

PARC JARDINS DU MONDE ●
With Japanese, Mediterranean and English gardens, as well as a bamboo labyrinth and more, the Parc Jardins du Monde certainly lives up to its name. *5, Avenue des Fleurs de la Paix | July/Aug daily 10am–8pm, Sept–June 10am–6pm | www. jardinsdumonde.com*

LOW BUDGET

▶ Even Ré has some cheap places to see: climb up ⤴ *Saint-Martin's bell tower (July/Aug daily 10am–11.30pm, Sept–Dec and Feb–June 10–sunset)*! A fantastic panorama can be enjoyed from the highest point on the island for just 1.70 euros.

▶ Crossing the Old Port in La Rochelle to Minime on the little *bus de mer boats (www.rtcr.fr)* costs 2 euros and offers a good view of the town from the water.

FOOD & DRINK

LE CARRELET

Fish dishes, seafood and regional specialities. *Daily | 56, Front de Mer | tel. 05 46 38 60 40 |* Moderate

L'ÉTOILE DE LA MER

Tuck into everything from *foie gras* to crab. *Closed Tue evening and Wed | 2, Rue de l'Étoile de la Mer | tel. 05 46 05 02 35 |* Moderate

SPORTS & BEACHES

The main beach is the 2km (1¼mi)-long *Grande Conche* where you can go sailing, jet-skiing, kayaking, kitesurfing, surfing and diving. Boat trips available to Ré, Oléron and Aix.

WHERE TO STAY

BEAU RIVAGE

At one end of the bay with a view of the sea and the estuary. *22 rooms | 9 Façade de Foncillon | tel. 05 46 39 43 10 | www.hotel-beau-rivage-royan.com |* Budget–Moderate

INFORMATION

1, Boulevard de la Grandière | tel. 05 46 23 00 00 | www.royan-tourisme.com

WHERE TO GO

LA PALMYRE (130 B4) *(D9)*

The resort La Palmyre (pop. 700) lies 17km (10½mi) northwest of Royan on the coast surrounded by a pine forest planted in the 19th century covering more than 30mi². Sandbanks enclose the sheltered bay *Bonne Anse,* that is especially suitable for families. There are also beaches for surfers and a nudist area. La Palmyre is linked to the village *La Tremblade,* that is famous for its oyster farms, by a 35km (22mi) cycle path. The lighthouse, Phare de la Coubre, is on the headland nearby. Information: *2, Avenue de Royan | tel. 05 46 22 41 07 | www.la-palmyre-les-mathes.com*

The lighthouse Phare de la Coubre protects the mouth of the Gironde near Royan

SAINT-PALAIS-SUR-MER (130 B5) *(D9)*

The fine sandy beaches, elegant Belle Époque villas and its attractive location on the Gironde estuary are all plus points of this small but lively resort (pop. 3400), 6km (3¾mi) to the northwest of La Rochelle. Information: *1, Avenue de la République | tel. 05 46 23 22 58 | www.saint-palais-sur-mer.com*

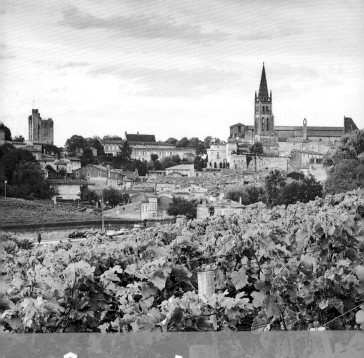

CÔTE D'ARGENT

250km (155mi) of sandy beach are a good enough argument for a holiday on the Côte d'Argent, the 'Silver Coast'. This strip between the Gironde estuary and the mouth of the Adour near Bayonne owes its name to the glitter of the sun on the sea.

Inland from the coast lies Europe's largest area of forest covering more than 3800mi². In the early 19th century pines were planted to stop the dunes from drifting further inland and the wetlands were drained.

The lakes a little way in from the coast are an ideal alternative for swimming and watersports to the Atlantic that often shows itself from its untamed side. Many towns and villages are divided into two with one part on a lake and one on the sea. Europe's highest dune, the Dune du Pilat is particularly impressive, rising to a height of 114–117m (374–383ft). It offers a fantastic view of the coast and Arcachon Bay that is perfect for swimming, being a miniature inland sea, as well as for farming oysters of exceptional quality. Apart from water that gave the Aquitaine region its name, wine also plays an important role. Most wines today are suitably produced in the various famous châteaux in Médoc, Haut-Médoc and in the area around Bordeaux.

Photo: Saint-Émilion

Water, woods and wine: endless beaches, powerful breakers and châteaux further inland attract swimmers, surfers and bon vivants

ARCACHON

[132 A4) *(◻ D12)* **This lively resort (pop. 12,000), that is like a big fairground at the height of summer, is right on huge Arcachon Bay that covers 60mi². With is promenade packed with restaurants and the pedestrianised Rue Maréchal-de-Lattre-de-Tassigny with cafés, boutiques** and ice cream parlours, it is difficult to believe that the first tourists in Arcachon were those with respiratory problems who came to breathe in the sea air and the smell of the pine trees.

Aristocrats and artists also found the spa fashionable after Napoleon III holidayed here in 1863. The 7km (4½mi)-long beach and the entertainments for children make this little town ideal for families.

BASILIQUE NOTRE DAME

The INSIDER TIP *Chapelle des Marins*, an 18th-century seaman's chapel, is perhaps more interesting than the 19th-centuy church due to all the votive pictures and buoys which decorate it.

Playful 19th-century architecture: a house in Arcachon's Ville d'Hiver

VILLE D'ÉTÉ

The 'Summer Town' at the foot of the hill between the pretty station and the promenade along the bank is bursting with life. Boats for Cap Ferret and tours around Arcachon Bay – to Île aux Oiseaux, for example – depart from the main beach.

The roulette ball has been spinning in the casino near the beach since 1903.

VILLE D'HIVER ★

The wooded 'Winter Town' where, from the late 19th century onwards, the wealthy from Bordeaux who suffered from ill health built their houses, is a complete mixture of fanciful architectural styles. There were three distinct phases of development: the 'pioneers' from the 1860s with their solid buildings making generous use of wood, the 'mad-hatters' from the 1870s to the Belle Époque with exotic and fantasy-like elements, and the 'modest' builders of the 1920s. The streets curve gently to break the wind. Protected in this way, the vegetation is Mediterranean in character. The ● ☀ *Observatoire Sainte-Cécile,* an iron structure which Gustave Eiffel was also involved in building, provides a good view over the area. There are 75 steps to the top.

CAP PEREIRE

Excellent fish specialities and sushi can be enjoyed here on a lovely ☀ terrace with a view over Arcachon Bay. *Closed Oct–March Mon/Tue | 1, Avenue du Parc Pereire | tel. 05 56 83 24 01 | www.restaurantcappereire.com | Moderate*

CAFÉ DE LA PLAGE (CHEZ PIERRE)

Very good fish and seafood on the promenade. *Daily | 1, Boulevard Veyrier Montagnères | tel. 05 56 22 52 94 | www.cafedelaplage.com | Moderate*

CHEZ YVETTE

An institution in Arcachon where both tourists and locals congregate. Delicious oysters from its own farm and other seafood can be found on the menu. *Daily | 59, Boulevard du Général Leclerc | tel. 05 56 83 05 11 | Moderate*

SHOPPING

A market is held daily (in winter Mon, Wed, Sun) from 8am–1pm in the market hall.

SPORTS & BEACHES

Plage Pereire is some 3km (2mi) long with the promenade running alongside and has a number of playgrounds, a skatepark and lawned areas. Youngsters head for the *Plage du Moulleau* and surfers for the *Plage des Arbousiers* to the west. Several companies in the marina cater for surfers, rowers, divers and jet skiers and have motorboats and catamarans for hire. Kayak rentals and trips are available from *Arcachon Kayak Adventure (Port de Plaisance | Centre Nautique Pierre Malet | www.arcachonkayak.com)*. There is a *tennis club* (20 sand courts, 2 inside courts) in *Parc Pereire (7, Avenue du Parc)*, a footpath that leads all the way around Arcachon Bay and an 18-hole golf course at *Golf International d'Arcachon (35, Boulevard d'Arcachon | tel. 05 56 54 44 00 | golfarcachon.org/fr)*. And if you fancy paddling across the bay standing up, then *Surf en Pays de Buch (tel. 06 80 05 46 95 | www.sup-arcachon.com)* is the right address. Here you can also book **INSIDER TIP** guided outings for stand-up paddlers to the oysters beds or past the Dune du Pilat.

ENTERTAINMENT

The *Club Le Scotch* belongs to the *Casino (163, Boulevard de la Plage)*. *L'Escorida (177, Boulevard de la Plage)* is equally chic.

WHERE TO STAY

HOTEL DE LA PLAGE
Medium category hotel near the beach with small rooms but friendly service. *53 rooms | 10, Avenue Nelly de Deganne | tel. 05 56 83 06 23 | www.hotelarcachon.com | Expensive*

⭐ **Dune du Pilat**
The view from the top of Europe's highest dune is an experience not to be missed → p. 68

⭐ **Biscarrosse**
More than just the sea: take a swim in the lake too → p. 68

⭐ **Ville d'Hiver in Arcachon**
The playful designs of the villas reflect the glory of an era when the rich and beautiful from Bordeaux came here to unwind → p. 66

⭐ **Pauillac**
A 'château crawl' for wine lovers → p. 80

⭐ **Saint-Émilion**
This wine village has all the charms of France rolled into one → p. 77

⭐ **Courant d'Huchet**
The river and jungle-like vegetation of this nature reserve make it one of the most beautiful parts of *les Landes* → p. 79

⭐ **Musée d'Art Contemporain CAPC**
Avant-garde art in an old harbour warehouse in Bordeaux → p. 72

⭐ **Phare de Cordouan**
Europe's oldest lighthouse still in use in the Gironde estuary → p. 83

MARCO POLO HIGHLIGHTS

RESIDHOME PLAZZA

This stylish apartment hotel with modern furnishings is 200m from the beach. There are 89 one-roomed studios and flats with separate kitchens. *49–51 bis, Avenue Lamartine | tel. 05 57 15 48 00 | www.resid home.com | Expensive*

GRAND HOTEL RICHELIEU

The glamour of the olden days on the beach where Empress Elisabeth of Austria once stayed. *45 rooms | 185, Boulevard de la Plage | tel. 05 56 83 16 50 | www.grand-hotel-richelieu.com | Moderate–Expensive*

THALAZUR

Thalassotherapy centre and hotel. *94 rooms | Avenue du Parc | tel. 05 57 72 06 66 | arcachon.thalazur.fr | Moderate*

INFORMATION

Esplanade Georges Pompidou | tel. 05 57 52 97 97 | www.arcachon.com

WHERE TO GO

CAP FERRET (132 A4) (*W D12*)

Pointe du Cap Ferret is at the southern end of a spit that encloses the Bassin d'Arcachon from the north. Its 53m (173ft)-high ⚲ *lighthouse (July/Aug daily 10am–7.30pm, April–June and Sept 10am–12.30pm and 2pm–6.30pm, Oct–March Wed–Sun 2pm–5pm)* offers wonderful views – but you'll have to climb the 258 steps first! Information: *1, Avenue du Général de Gaulle | tel. 05 56 03 94 49 | www.lege-capferret.com*

DUNE DU PILAT ★ ● ⚲
(132 A4) (*W D12*)

Avoid the crowds which build up from 10am onwards around the souvenir stalls before they stagger up the 170 steps fixed in the sand to the top of Europe's largest dune, 10km (6mi) south of Arcachon (114–117m/374–383ft; almost 3km/2mi long). The view over pine forests and white sandbanks to the deep-blue sea and along the ridge of the dune is so fantastic that you should not be put off by the car-parking charge of 4 euros an hour. There are lots of campsites right on the sea to the south of the dune. Information: *Rond-Point du Figuier/2, Avenue Ermitage | Pyla-sur-Mer | tel. 05 56 54 02 22 | www.tourisme-latestedebuch.fr*

BISCARROSSE

(132 A5) (*W D13*) ★ **A seaside and lakeside resort in one: Biscarrosse (pop. 13,000) is divided into three: Plage, Ville and the watersports eldorado Biscarrosse Lac at the southern end of Lac Nord.**

A cycle path connects the different parts through the slightly hilly countryside. Two canals link Lac Sud, Petit Lac de Biscarrosse and Lac Nord. By connecting the coast with the inland region in such a way, a perfect holiday environment has been created. When the Atlantic is too rough you can head for the northern lake where the gently sloping banks are ideal for children too. Watersports enthusiasts have

LOW BUDGET

▶ Entrance to the permanent exhibitions in the *Musée d'Aquitaine* and the *Musée des Beaux Arts* in Bordeaux is free.

▶ Why not visit one of the famous wine-producers in Médoc? Almost all tours are free and you really learn a lot about viniculture.

At the top of the Dune du Pilat between the pine forest and the ocean

sheer endless possibilities. With its market, boutiques, cafés and 10km (6mi) of beach, Biscarrosse-Plage has all the amenities of a seaside resort.

SIGHTSEEING

MUSÉE DE L'HYDRAVIATION

Seaplanes were designed and tested in Biscarrosse from 1930–55 and their history can be traced in this museum. *332, Avenue Louis Bréguet | Biscarrosse-Ville | July/Aug daily 10am–7pm, Sept–June Wed–Mon 2pm–6pm | www.asso-hydraviation. com*

MUSÉE DES TRADITIONS

Presenting the town's history and traditions. *216, Avenue Louis Bréguet | Biscarrosse-Ville | July/Aug Mon–Sat 9.30am–7pm, Sun 2pm–6pm, June and Sept Tue–Sat 9am–noon and 2pm–6pm, mid Feb–May after enquiring in advance: tel. 05 58 78 77 37 | museetraditions.com*

FOOD & DRINK

INSIDER TIP L'IDYLLE CAFÉ PLAGE

A lovely mixture of a lounge bar and restaurant on the lakeside. Dig your toes into the (heaped up) sand at the Tapabar. The restaurant serves seafood and local wine from dawn 'til dusk – and all in the open air. *Daily | 18, Chemin de de Maguide | tel. 05 58 09 87 14 | www.lidylle-plage.com | Budget*

LE PARCOURS GOURMAND

Elegant dining in the golf club with a view of the green. *Closed Mon | Avenue du Golf | tel. 05 58 09 84 84 | Moderate*

LA PLAGE

Fresh seafood right on Biscarrosse-Plage. *May–Oct daily | Budget*

RESTAUMER

Fish and seafood with its own fish market. Correspondingly lively and informal at-

BISCARROSSE

mosphere. *March–Oct daily | 210, Avenue de la Plage | tel. 05 58 78 20 26 | www. restaumer.fr | Budget*

INSIDER TIP **LE SAINT-EX**

Traditional cuisine in a restaurant fitted out like a seaplane to honour the writer Antoine de Saint-Exupéry. The author of *The Little Prince* was a test pilot in Biscarrosse in the 1930s. *Mid June–Sept daily, otherwise closed in the evening | Place de l'Église Biscarrosse-Ville | tel. 05 58 78 16 16 | Budget–Moderate*

SHOPPING

Large daily market in Biscarrosse-Plage with regional produce, clothes and souvenirs.

SPORTS & BEACHES

Sailing, boats for hire, surfing, waterskiing, boat trips, land yachting, a beach club for children, diving, golf, rental bikes: there is virtually nothing that is not available … the southern-most section of the (unmanned) beach is reserved for nudists.

ENTERTAINMENT

L'Oceana (46, Rue du Grand Vivier | mid June–Sept daily, otherwise Fri/Sat) is a popular club in Biscarrosse-Plage. There is also a *casino (Boulevard des Sables)*.

WHERE TO STAY

CAMPSITES

Biscarrosse has seven 4-star sites. ☺ *Camping Domaine de la Rive (Route de Bordeaux | tel. 05 58 78 12 33 | www.larive. fr)* on Lac Nord has an outdoor and a heated indoor pool, a restaurant, supermarket and more than 800 pitches, and comes with a 'green' seal of approval.

HÔTEL LA CARAVELLE ☙

The only hotel in Biscarrosse-Lac with a view of the lake, beach and moorings Restaurant with regional cuisine. *11 rooms | 5314, Route des Lacs | tel. 05 58 09 82 67 | www.lacaravelle.fr | Moderate*

INSIDER TIP **LE COMPTOIR DES SABLES**

Lovely guesthouse 300m from the beach Thoughtfully furnished rooms with a lot of wood and attractively designed bath room areas, some with private terraces Spa facilities. *5 rooms | 34, Avenue de la Libération | Biscarrosse-Plage | tel. 05 58 78 35 20 | www.lecomptoirdessables.fr | Expensive*

INSIDER TIP **CÔTE & DUNE**

Stylish white wooden building with a view of the dunes and its own pool and spa The rooms have been decorated in a light coloured 'beach look' with ornamental driftwood. Each has its own balcony or terrace and overlooks the pool. A path leads directly to the beach. *5 rooms | 675 Avenue Gabriele D'Annunzio | Biscarrosse Plage | tel. 05 58 08 17 29 | www.cotedune. fr | Expensive*

HÔTEL LA FORESTIÈRE

The wood next to the hotel has gone but some spruce trees are still there, making this an attractive place to stay, albeit 800m from the sea. The 50 not very spacious rooms are grouped around a heated pool Own restaurant. *1300, Avenue du Pyla Biscarrosse-Plage | tel. 05 58 78 24 14 www.hotellaforestiere.com | Moderate*

HÔTEL LES VAGUES

Simple, welcoming hotel 300m from the beach in the pine forest. Own restaurant *29 rooms | 99, Rue des Iris | Biscarrosse Plage | tel. 05 58 83 98 10 | www.les vagues.com | Moderate*

BORDEAUX

MAP INSIDE BACK COVER
(132 C3) (⊞ E11) Bordeaux, the world's wine capital, the capital of Aquitaine and a Unesco World Heritage Site since 2007 not only has the best possible location between the châteaux and wide expanses of beach but it is a city with its own very special appeal.

The metropolis on the Garonne (pop. 235,000 or 660,000 in the Greater Bordeaux area) has been given a beauty treatment and now shows off its architectural heritage to the full. The 5000 Classicist listed buildings in the Old Town have been restored and their façades cleaned. Bit by bit, cars are disappearing from the centre. The Old Town has an underground system of tunnels linking the multi-storey car parks; several streets are only open to residents and pedestrians. And if you get tired, take one of the 'green' bicycle taxis – rickshaws crisscross the centre along fixed routes.

The city owes it harmonious overall appearance to its remodelling in the 18th century after Bordeaux became rich thanks to the wine trade with England. Nowadays, Bordeaux has a cultural life expected of any major city as well as excellent shops.

The monument to the Girondists on the Place des Quinconces

WHERE TO START?

There are several underground car parks in the Old Town. Head for the **Esplanade des Quinconces** as most important sights are between here, the cathedral and the Garonne. The city centre is closed to traffic on the first Sun in the month. If you arrive by train, take tram C from the Gare Saint-Jean along the Garonne to the Quinconces stop opposite the Office de Tourisme.

Reaching up to heaven: Tour Pey-Berland – the cathedral bell tower

SIGHTSEEING

CATHÉDRALE SAINT-ANDRÉ

The Royal Gate depicting the 10 Apostles, the Resurrection and the Last Judgment and the North Gate with the Last Supper, the Ascension and the Triumph of Christ are well worth seeing. *Place Jean Moulin*

ESPLANADE DES QUINCONCES

This square, extending over more than 30 acres – one of the largest in Europe – was laid out in 1818–28 on the banks of the river. The column, almost 50m (164ft) high, with its statue of liberty was completed in 1902 and commemorates the Girondists who were executed. Two fountains decorated with bronze sculptures play at its base. The two other statues are of the writer Michel de Montaigne and the political thinker Charles de Secondat, Baron de Montesquieu.

MUSÉE D'AQUITAINE

The history of Aquitaine can be traced in this museum which includes archeological finds and sections on wine growing and oyster farming. *20, Cours Pasteur | Tue–Sun 11am–6pm*

MUSÉE D'ART CONTEMPORAIN CAPC ★

Excellent collection of contemporary art. Some 700 seminal drawings, paintings, photographs, installations and sculptures created from the 1970s onwards are exhibited in the Centre d'Arts Plastiques Contemporains, housed in a warehouse from the early 19th century – the Entrepô Laîné – that itself is well worth seeing. *Rue Ferrère | Tue–Sun 11am–6pm (Wed 8pm) | www.capc-bordeaux.fr*

MUSÉE DES BEAUX ARTS

Paintings from the 17th–20th centuries, including works by Rubens, Matisse

Picasso and Renoir. *20, Cours d'Albret | projected reopening after renovation: late 2012*

LE MUSÉE DU VIN ET DES NÉGOCIANTS

Of course Bordeaux has its own wine museum that recounts the history of wine growing. And after the theoretical comes the practical! *41, Rue Borie | Fri–Wed 10am–6pm, Thu 10am–10pm | www. mvnb.fr*

PLACE DE LA BOURSE

The elegant Place de la Bourse on the river promenade is flanked by the stock exchange on the north and the former custom's house (not the Custom's Museum) on the south side. A fountain with the Three Graces from the 19th century is a decorative central feature.

PLACE DE LA COMÉDIE

The magnificent *Grand Théâtre* (tickets: *tel. 05 56 00 85 95*), built in 1773–80 in the Neo-Classicist style, dominates the square with the *Hôtel de Rolly*, also designed by the architect Victor Louis opposite.

TOUR PEY-BERLAND ☼

A lovely view of the city can be enjoyed from the viewing platform on the 47m (154ft)-high bell tower adjoining Saint-André cathedral. *July/Aug daily 10am–7pm, June and Sept 10am–6pm, Oct–May 10am–12.30pm and 2pm–5pm*

FOOD & DRINK

INSIDER TIP ▶ BAUD & MILLET

Almost everything revolves around cheese in this restaurant and the adjoining cheese shop with 200 types on offer. You can find the matching wine downstairs in the cellar. *Closed Sun | 19, Rue Huguerie | tel. 05 56 79 05 77 | www.baudetmillet.fr | Budget*

INSIDER TIP ▶ CAFÉ ANDRÉE PUTMAN

Excellent food is served in this stylish, well located café-restaurant in the Musée CAPC. *Closed Mon and evenings | 7, Rue Ferrère | tel. 05 56 44 71 61 | Budget*

CAFÉ DU THÉÂTRE

Delicious regional specialities such as braised shoulder of lamb with apricots can be found on the menu in this unpretentious bistro-style café-restaurant. *Closed Sun/Mon | 3, Square Jean Vauthier/Place Renaudel | tel. 05 57 95 77 20 | www.cafe dutheatre-bordeaux.com | Moderate*

LE CHAPON FIN

This gourmets' paradise, where the artist Henri de Toulouse-Lautrec and King Edward VII once dined, is an institution. The head chef, Nicolas Frion, a pupil of Paul Bocuse's, advocates a creative but classically French cuisine. *Closed Sun/Mon | 5, Rue Montesquieu | tel. 05 56 79 10 10 | www.chapon-fin.com | Expensive*

CHEZ DUPONT

Regional classics from *foie gras* to mussel dishes in the trendy Quartier des Chartrons. *Closed Sun/Mon | 45, Rue Notre Dame | tel. 05 56 81 49 59 | Budget*

CHEZ JEAN

The sleek interior design of this brasserie allows you to focus on the classical dishes of the southwest region such as the excellent fish specialities and the local wines. Good homemade burgers are also available. *Daily | Place du Parlement | tel. 05 56 44 44 43 | www.restaurant.chezjean bordeaux.fr | Budget*

INSIDER TIP ▶ LA ROBE

Wine from but not only for women. The wine decanted in this winebar and restaurant is exclusively made by women. Specialities from the southwest of France are also served. *Daily | 3, Quai Louis XVIII | tel. 05 586 69 04 80 | www.la-robe.fr | Budget–Moderate*

LE SAINT-JAMES ☆

Michel Portos' restaurant with 2 Michelin Stars in Bouliac to the southeast of the city does not fall short in any way of its wonderful view over Bordeaux. A luxury hotel with 18 rooms and suites also belongs to this complex located in the midst

central feature in the restaurant. *Daily | 6, Rue Porte de la Monnaie | tel. 05 56 91 56 37 | www.latupina.com | Expensive*

SHOPPING

The *Rue Sainte-Catherine* pedestrian precinct is the top address for fashions (e. g. *Galeries Lafayette)* and souvenirs. *Rue Notre-Dame* in the Quartier des Chartrons is home to many antique dealers. Within

Haute culture in Bordeaux's opera house: the Neo-Classicist Grand Théâtre

of vineyards. *Restaurant closed Sun/Mon | 3, Place Camille Hostein | Bouliac | tel. 05 56 44 27 68 | www.saintjames-bouliac. com | Expensive*

LA TUPINA

Regional delicacies ranging from caviar from Aquitaine to duck from *les Landes*. A cauldron (called a *tupina* in Basque) in which a hearty stew is usually simmering away, creates a rustic atmosphere in winter. It hangs over an open fire that forms a

the 'golden triangle' *(Allées de Tourny/ Cours Clemenceau/Cours de l'Intendance)*, there are a number of well-stocked wine shops (e.g. *Passavant | 44, Allées de Tourny)*. Wine tasting can be enjoyed in the ● *Maison du Vin de Bordeaux (1, Cours de 30 Juillet)* which also holds wine-making courses, and wine can be bought in the adjoining vinotheque. A **INSIDER TIP** *food and delicatessen market* is held on Sun opposite the war cruiser 'Colbert' on Quai des Chartrons near Cours Martinique or

CÔTE D'ARGENT

the Garonne. The *market* is open Tue–Sun in the *Halles Les Capucins*.

ENTERTAINMENT

Live jazz and blues are played in *Le Blueberry (61, Rue Camille Sauvageau)* and *Le Comptoir du Jazz (57 ter, Quai de Paludate)*. The *Opéra National de Bordeaux (tel. 05 56 00 85 95 | www.opera-bordeaux.com)* has a very good reputation and plays in three venues: opera is performed in the *Grand Théâtre*, operetta in *Théâtre Fémina (10, Rue de Grassi)* and symphony concerts in *Palais des Sports (Place de la Ferme de Richemont)*. Techno and lounge music can be heard in *Dame de Shanghaï (Bassins à Flot | Rue E. Faure)*. The submarine base nearby, built by the Germans in World War II, where *Bar Le Café Maritime (Bassins à Flot | Quai Lalande)* can also be found, has developed into a popular place for a night out.

WHERE TO STAY

BLUE LODGE
Charming and well cared for guesthouse near the city centre with a garden and 4 individually furnished rooms. Book well in advance for the summer! *70, Rue de Ségur | tel. 06 78 25 85 83 | www.bluelodgeinbordeaux.com | Moderate*

GRAND HÔTEL
The best hotel in town in the best location opposite the opera house has 150 opulently furnished rooms with every conceivable luxury from flat screen TVs to marble bathrooms. *2–5, Place de la Comédie | tel. 05 57 30 44 44 | www.rghbordeaux.com | Expensive*

LA MAISON DU LIERRE
A cosy hotel in an ancient building with a garden, located in the 'golden triangle'.

12 rooms | 57, Rue Huguerie | tel. 05 56 51 92 71 | www.maisondulierre.com | Moderate

HÔTEL DES QUATRES SŒURS
The rooms are plain but bright and friendly – and the location cannot be topped! That makes parking difficult but there is an underground car park nearby. *34 rooms | 6, Cours du 30 Juillet | tel. 05 57 81 19 20 | www.hotel-bordeaux-centre.com | Moderate*

LA TOUR INTENDANCE
This hotel with its stylish contemporary furnishings, lovely wooden floors and partially exposed stone walls, is right in the thick of things. *24 rooms | 16, Rue de la Vieille Tour | tel. 05 56 44 56 56 | www.hotel-tour-intendance.com | Moderate–Expensive*

LA VILLA BORDELAISE
10 mins. from the Old Town, this small hotel in a beautifully restored building some 100 years old, with a small garden and terrace, appeals more to those seeking a bit of peace and quiet. *2 rooms | 48, Rue des Frères Faucher | tel. 05 56 58 27 63 | www.lescinqsens-bordeaux.com | Expensive*

INFORMATION

12, Cours du 30 Juillet | tel. 05 56 00 66 00 | www.bordeaux-tourisme.com

WHERE TO GO

BLAYE (132 C2) (*ⵍ E10*)
A vast citadel completed in 1689 is the main attraction in this little town (pop. 5000) 45km (28mi) north of Bordeaux on the Gironde. Inside the citadel a craft village and eateries have been established. Otherwise everything in Blaye revolves around wine, especially red wine.

The *Maison du Vin de Blaye (12, Cours Vauban | Mon–Sat 8.30am–12.30pm and 2pm–6.30pm | www.vin-blaye.com)* provides a good overview.

birthday to the library tower on his estate to find more peace to write. For nine years he did not leave the tower. The result: three volumes of his famous *Essais*. These

The charming wine-producing town of Saint-Émilion is well worth a visit

LA BRÈDE (132 C4) (*M E12*)

Château de la Brède (May/June and Sept/ Oct Wed–Mon 2pm–6.30pm, July/Aug 9.30am–6-45pm | www.chateaulabrede. com), in the little village of the same name (pop. 3500), 18km (11mi) south of Bordeaux, is where the social commentator and political thinker Charles Louis de Secondat, Baron de la Brède et de Montesquieu (1689–1755) grew up. The moated castle surrounded by a park is still in the family's ownership. Some of the rooms are open to the public.

CHÂTEAU MONTAIGNE (133 D3) (*M G11*)

Michel de Montaigne (1533–1592) retired from the pressures of life on his 38th

have led to the tower, some 50km (30mi) to the east of Bordeaux, becoming a much-visited site today. The château burnt down in the 19th century and has since been rebuilt; the tower has been retained. *July/ Aug daily 10am–6.30pm, May/June and Sept/Oct Wed–Sun 10–noon and 2pm–6.30pm, otherwise 5.30pm, closed Jan. | www.chateau-montaigne.com*

MARTILLAC (132 C3) (*M E12*)

Wine doesn't just taste good, it makes you look good too – according to the 'wine therapy spa hotel' ● *Les Sources de Caudalie (49 rooms and suites | tel. 05 57 83 83 83 | www.sources-caudalie.com | Expensive)*. Holidaymakers can wine and dine between the vineyards just a few miles south of Bordeaux in Château Smith-Haut Lafitte near Martillac and enjoy a health and beauty treatment at the same time, such as a 'peeling à la Sauvignon' or a 'wine massage'.

SAINT-ÉMILION ★
(133 D3) (*Ø F11*)

This small town (pop. 3000) 40km (25mi) east of Bordeaux is spread across two hills. The delightful, traffic-free Old Town (packed in summer) and the wine merchants with their wide range of wares are just as much part and parcel of the attractions as the subterranean *Église Monnolithe* hewn into the rock, the *catacombs* and the *Chapelle de la Trinité* (9th–13th century).

There are several dozen wineries in the vicinity – addresses are available from the Office du Tourisme. Regional fare and a wide selection of wines can be found in the restaurant and brasserie *Amelia Canta (daily | 2, Place de l'Église Monolithe | tel. 05 57 74 48 03 | www.ameliacanta.com | Budget)*. The Michelin Star chef Philippe Etchebest manages the restaurant kitchen at the elegant *Hostellerie de Plaisance (17 rooms, 4 suites | restaurant closed Sun/Mon | Place du Clocher | tel. 05 57 55 07 55 | www.hostellerie-plaisance.com | Expensive)*, housed in the walls of the former monastery. INSIDER TIP ▶ *Château Franc Mayne (9 rooms | 14, La Gomerie | tel. 05 57 24 62 61 | www.chateaufranc mayne.com | Expensive)* is beautifully furnished and guests can enjoy the privilege of sampling the château's own wines. Information: *Place des Créneaux | tel. 05 57 55 28 28 | www.saint-emilion-tourisme.com*

SAINT-MACAIRE
(133 D4) (*Ø F12*)

This little medieval town (pop. 5700) a good 40km (25mi) southeast of Bordeaux is surrounded by vineyards. *Saint-Sauveur*

church from the 11th century, the *Place du Mercadiou (market Thu)* and the ruins of a 12th-century Benedictine abbey are delight. Information: *8, Rue du Canton | tel. 05 56 63 32 14 | www.saintmacaire.fr*

MIMIZAN

(134 C2) (*Ø D13–14*) **The fame of this part of the coastline found its beginnings in the 1920s in this pretty holiday resort (pop. 8000) south of the Étang d'Aureilhan.**

Coco Chanel was among the first summer guests. Like Winston Churchill, Charlie Chaplin and Salvador Dalí she stayed at the Duke of Westminster's lakeside hunting lodge, Château Woolsack (privately owned). 6km (3¾mi) lie between Mimizan-Bourg and Mimizan-Plage although they are slowly joining up. *Plage* is an idyllic holiday location with a pedestrian precinct, a promenade along the riverbank, a comprehensive range of watersports facilities and five wide beaches. The 7km (4½mi)-long watercourse, the Courant de Mimizan, links the lake with the sea and divides Mimizan's 10km (6mi)-long beach into a northern and southern section. There are more than 300 types of plant on the 'Flower Promenade' *(Rue du Lac)*. Mimizan-Bourg is where the municipal offices are concentrated as well as industry in the form of a paper factory that, unfortunately, can be smelt from miles around. Thanks to its range of facilities for children, Mimizan received the 'Station Kid' award (see: 'Travel with Kids').

SIGHTSEEING

BENEDICTINE ABBEY
In the mid 17th century, the Benedictine monks abandoned the abbey situated on the road between Mimizan and Mimizan-

Plage that had been so important in the Middle Ages. 100 years later it was buried under a 'migrating' dune – only the bell tower stuck out of the sand. With its carved portal from the 13th century, it is now a Unesco World Heritage Site. An exhibition traces the history of the abbey and the region *(open by appointment: tel. 05 58 09 00 61). Rue de l'Abbaye | mid June–mid Sept Mon–Sat 10am–12.30pm and 2pm–5pm | musee.mimizan.com*

MUSÉE D'HISTOIRE DE MIMIZAN
The local museum documents the history of the area, how the forest was used and professions such as that of the sawmill worker, the gum-tapper and the donkey driver. *Rue de l'Abbaye | mid June–mid Sept Mon–Sat, otherwise Mon–Fri after making an appointment in advance, tel. 05 58 09 00 61 at 10am, 11am, 2pm, 3pm and 4pm*

FOOD & DRINK

LE BISTROT DE LA MER
Seafood and fish in rustic surroundings with a billiard table. *Daily | 8, Avenue Maurice Martin | tel. 05 58 09 08 56 | Budget*

ILE DE MALTE
Quality cuisine. The walls are decorated with old views of Mimizan. *Daily | 5, Rue du Casino | tel. 05 58 82 48 15 | iledemalte-mimizan.com | Moderate*

A NOSTE ⁂
Fish and seafood with a wonderful view of the beach. *Daily | 7, Avenue de la Côte d'Argent | tel. 05 58 09 31 34 | www.anoste.fr | Budget*

INSIDER TIP ▶ LA TABLE DE LA FERME
Regional fare, moderate prices, lovely garden. *Daily | 31, Avenue Maurice Martin | tel. 05 58 09 27 81 | Moderate*

SHOPPING

A *food market* is held every day in the market hall; the *evening market* selling arts and crafts, clothes and regional produce is on Thu on the Place du Marché.

SPORTS & ACTIVITIES

Apart from virtually all types of sport on or in water, riding and golf also belong to the extensive range of things to do.

ENTERTAINMENT

No seaside resort does without its gambling den. In addition to the *casino* in Rue du Casino, popular clubs include *Le Dark Club (2, Avenue de la Jetée), Le Mambo (8, Rue Assolant, Lefèvre et Lotti)* and *Les Bains de Minuit (14, Rue Assolant, Lefèvre et Lotti)*.

WHERE TO STAY

CAMPING CLUB MARINA-LANDES
In a pine forest with access to the beach; shops, swimming pool, restaurant and a children's playground. *573 pitches, several chalets and bungalows | Rue Marina | Plage Sud | tel. 05 58 09 12 66 | www.marinalandes.com*

HÔTEL L'ÉMERAUDE DES BOIS
The hotel (and its restaurant) are on the banks of the Courant, just a 5-min. drive from the beach and the town. *15 rooms | 66/68, Avenue de Courant | Plage Sud | tel. 05 58 09 05 28 | www.emeraudedesbois.com | Moderate*

HÔTEL DE FRANCE
Simple, friendly and close to the beach. *21 rooms | 18, Avenue de la Côte d'Argent | tel. 05 58 09 09 01 | www.hoteldefrance-mimizan.com | Moderate*

Ideal for boating: the Courant d'Huchet, the most beautiful river in *les Landes*

ECOLODGE SEGOSA ☺

A former barn has been converted and furnished to exacting enviromental standard to create this small hotel in the little village of Saint-Paul-en-Born, 10 mins. from the coast. With natural thermal regulation, the use of locally sourced natural materials and renewable energy sources, the owners have gone way beyond doing away with clean towels every day to ensure a sustainable economic management. But guests do not have to do without any creature comforts or style. *14 rooms | Route de Mezos | Saint-Paul-en-Born | tel. 06 89 49 58 84 | www.ecolodge-segosa.com | Moderate*

INFORMATION

38, Avenue Maurice Martin | tel. 05 58 09 11 20 | www.mimizan-tourism.com

WHERE TO GO

CONTIS-PLAGE (134 C2) (*Ø C–D14*)
23km (14mi) to the south of Mimizan is this little resort where the Courant de Contis meets the sea. The beautiful, mile-long beaches are ideal for a peaceful seaside holiday. The ☼ *lighthouse (July/Aug Thu 10.30am–12.30pm and 2.30pm–4.30pm),* built in 1862 and the only one between Cap Ferret and Capbreton, is the pride of the village. After climbing the 183 steps, you have a wonderful paroramic view along the coast and across the forest inland. Information: *Avenue de l'Océan | tel. 05 58 42 89 80 | www.contis-tourisme.com*

COURANT D'HUCHET ★
(134 C3) (*Ø C15*)
This nature reserve around the Courant d'Huchet is a good 40km (25mi) south

of Mimizan. The little river flows through a forested landscape and enters the sea near Huchet. Guided canoe tours and hikes are available from *Pichelèbe*. To book: *tel. 05 58 48 75 39 | www.batelier.com*

LÉON (134 C3) (*
ﾑ
 D15*)

This pretty holiday resort (pop. 1500) 40km (25mi) south of Mimizan is on the Lac de Léon and 7km (4½mi) from the sea. The comprehensive range of activities on offer (golf, surfing and sailing schools, riding and swimming in the lake) is perfect for families with children. The campsite *Lou Puntaou (1315, Avenue du Lac | tel. 05 58 48 74 30 | www.loupuntaou.com)* with 391 pitches, a large outdoor swimming pool, children's club, bar and restaurant is on the lakeside. Information: *65, Place Jean Bap-tiste Courtiau | tel. 05 58 48 76 03 | www.ot-leon.fr*

MOLIETS-ET-MAA (134 C3) (*
ﾑ
 C15*)

Another relatively quiet, family-friendly resort south of Mimizan (47km/29mi) is Moliets-et-Maa. Its attractions include a lake, lots of pine trees and the beach at Moliets-Plage just 2.5km (1½mi) away. Moliets-et-Maa has an attractive centre with pretty old buildings, a church and a chapel. The sports and leisure activity programme is extensive. There are hiking trails through the forest, fishing grounds, a golf course, an aerial ropeway, riding clubs, tennis courts, a skatepark and of course every conceivable type of watersport. Information: *Rue du Général Caunègre | tel. 05 58 48 56 58 | www.moliets. com*

SABRES (135 D2) (*
ﾑ
 E14*)

It is well worth travelling the 45km (28mi) inland to the open-air museum *Écomusée de la Grande Lande (June–mid Sept daily, train 10.10am–12.10pm and 2pm–4.40pm every 40 mins., last train 6pm, April/May* *and mid Sept–Oct Mon–Sat, trains every 40 mins., 2pm–4.40pm, Sun 10.10am– 4.40pm | www.parc-landes-de-gascogne. fr)*. A historical railway takes you from Sabres right into the marsh and moorland of *les Landes* in the 19th-century. In the museum village *Marquèze*, watch farmers ploughing their fields with oxen, listen to the soothing sound of the watermill and smell the fresh bread in the baker's shop – a museum for all the senses.

VIEUX-BOUCAU-LES-BAINS/ PORT D'ALBRET (134 B–C3) (*
ﾑ
 C15*)

This village 54km (33½mi) south of Mimizan was a not unimportant port, known as Port d'Albret, until the largest river in *les Landes*, the Adour, was diverted to Bayonne in the 16th century. Vieux-Boucau (pop. 1400) is now a lively holiday destination with attractive half-timbered buildings in its traffic-free centre, a lake, dunes, new holiday houses and the promenade *Le Mail*. La Côte d'Argent *(36 rooms | 4, Grand'Rue | tel. 05 58 48 13 17 | www.lacotedargent-vieuxboucau. fr | Budget)* is a pleasant hotel in the pedestrian precinct. Information: *11, Mail André Rigal | tel. 05 58 48 13 47 | www.ot-vieux-boucau.fr*

PAUILLAC

**(132 B1) (*
ﾑ
 E10*)** ★ **The Médoc peninsula on the western bank of the Gironde is anchored in the minds of every lover of red wine the whole world over.**

Visitors to the largest village, Pauillac (pop. 5200), with its 23 châteaux, midway between the coast and Bordeaux, should have a car with as big a boot as possible! There is also a lovely beach, an elegant marina and many opportunities for watersports.

SIGHTSEEING

CHÂTEAUX ●

Almost all the châteaux are open to the public except in the grape-picking season. Visits must always be booked in advanced,

Châteaux | tel. 05 56 59 24 39 | www. chateau-gaudin.fr); in this family-run business you can INSIDER TIP cork and label a bottle yourself, for which you are given a 'diploma' and you can keep the bottle as a souvenir.

Château Mouton-Rothschild: clear elegant lines rather than folksy kitsch

either directly at the winery or through the Office du Tourisme. The most famous places include *Château Lafite-Rothschild (fax only 05 56 59 26 83 | www.lafite. com), Château Latour (tel. 05 56 73 19 80 | www.chateau-latour.fr), Château Pichon-Longueville (tel. 05 56 73 17 17 | chateau pichonlongueville.com), Château Mouton-Rothschild (tel. 05 56 73 20 20 | www. mouton-rothschild.com),* the Rolls-Royce of all the châteaux with its own wine history museum, *Château Lynch-Bages (tel. 05 56 73 24 00 | www.lynchbages.com)* and *Château Gaudin (2/8, Route des*

PETIT MUSÉE DES AUTOMATES

This fascinating exhibition of mechanical toys is not just for children. *3, Rue Aristide Briand | July/Aug Tue–Sat 10am–1pm and 2pm–7pm, April–June and Sept 10am–12.30pm and 2.30pm–7pm, Oct–March Thu–Sat 10am–12.30pm and 2.30pm–7pm | museeautomatespauillac.jimdo.com*

FOOD & DRINK

INSIDER TIP CAFÉ LAVINAL

The owner of Château Lynch-Bages, Jean-Michel Cazes, bought and restored his native village of *Bages* south of Pauillac which had been virtually completely deserted. It now has a baker, shops and this restaurant which serves regional fare. *Closed Sun evenings | Place Desquet | tel. 05 57 75 00 09 | Moderate*

CORDEILLAN BAGES

Gourmet cuisine in the hotel of the same name that belongs to the Relais-&-Châteaux chain. The head chef, Jean-Luc Rocha, has now taken over from the legendary Thierry Marx. *Closed Sat lunchtime and Mon/Tue | Route des Châteaux | tel. 05 56 59 24 24 | www.cordeillanbages. com | Expensive*

Apart from wine, there is also a pretty *market (Sat mornings | Place du Marché)*. More than 300 of a total of 1500 Médoc varieties of wine are displayed and sold in the Office du Tourisme et du Vin – at the same price as at the châteaux.

CHÂTEAU POMYS VIN ET SÉJOUR

Those who don't want to drive after a wine tasting session, can stay in the winery itself. *10 rooms | Route de Poumeys Saint-Estèphe | tel. 05 56 59 73 44 | www. chateaupomys.com | Moderate*

HÔTEL DE FRANCE ET D'ANGLETERRE

This hotel with a pretty garden and a restaurant is on the Gironde estuary. *28 rooms | 3, Quai Albert Pichon | tel. 05 56 59 01 20 | www.hoteldefrance-angleterre. com | Budget*

La Verrerie | tel. 05 56 59 03 08 | www. pauillac-medoc.com

HOURTIN (132 A1) (*Ⓜ D10*)

This village (pop. 3250) 25km (15½mi) west of Pauillac is divided into *Plage*, *Lac* and the marina *Port*. The *Lac d'Hourtin et de Carcans,* the largest natural inland lake in France, is a mecca for watersports enthusiasts. Hourtin has been awarded the 'Station Kid' title thanks to its 24-acre, traffic-free 'children's island'. The hotel *Le Dauphin (17 rooms | 17, Place de l'Église | tel. 05 56 09 11 15 | www.le-dauphin.fr | Budget)* is highly commendable. The campsite *La Côte d'Argent (Rue d'Aquitaine | tel. 05 56 09 10 25 | www.cca33.com)*, 300m from the sea and 4km (2½mi) from the lake, has a pool, gym, children's club, lots of sports amenities and a restaurant. Information: *Place du Port | tel. 05 56 09 19 00 | www.hourtin-medoc.com*

LACANAU-OCÉAN (132 A2) (*Ⓜ D11*)

The more than 14km (8mi)-long beach with its high dunes, the Lac de Lacanau and dense pine forests are the plus points of this village (pop. 3400) a good 50km (30mi) to the southwest. Lacanau is one of the major seaside resorts on the Côte d'Argent offering every conceivable type of watersport, 3 golf courses, 3 riding schools and an extensive network of cycle paths and hiking trails. Information: *Place de l'Europe | tel. 05 56 03 21 01 | www. lacanau.com*

MONTALIVET-LES-BAINS
(130 B6) (*Ⓜ D10*)

This village (pop. 1900), almost 40km (25mi) to the northwest, has been popular among nudists since the 1950s. Apart from in dedicated holiday complexes, nude bathing is tolerated on the *Plage du Gressier*. Euronat *(Grayan-L'Hôpital | tel. 05 56 09 33 33 | www.euronat.fr)*. **INSIDER TIP** Europe's largest nudist colony.

is 5km (3mi) away and has its own thalassotherapy centre. Information: *62, Avenue de l'Océ-an | Vendays Montalivet | tel. 05 56 09 30 12 | www.ot-vendays-montalivet.fr*

PHARE DE CORDOUAN ★ ●
(130 B5) (*ꟼ D9*)

The 16th-century lighthouse in the Gironde estuary could once be reached on foot at low tide. Now it is washed by the waves

the round-trip takes 4 hours. *(Advance booking essential: Crosières La Sirène | tel. 06 81 84 47 80 | www.croisierelasirene. com). www.pharedecordouan.com*

SOULAC-SUR-MER
(130 B5) (*ꟼ D9*)

The most northerly seaside resort (pop. 2900) on the Côte d'Argent, a good 50km (30mi) north of Pauillac, combines all the plus points of the 'Silver Coast' – dunes,

A dining room right out in the ocean: inside the Phare de Cordouan

7km (4½mi) out to sea. It is the oldest traditional lighthouse in Europe still in operation today. Excursion boats take visitors to the 67.5m (222ft)-high tower which can be climbed (311 steps). On one of the floors is a chapel and, on anther, a royal suite, should the monarch have happened to drop by. 'Vedette Jules Verne' departs from Royan for the lighthouse;

the pine forest, the sea and a casino. The *Plage Centrale* is protected by a sandbank and groynes. *Océan Hôtel Amélie (21 rooms | tel. 05 56 09 78 05 | www.ocean hotelamelie.com | Moderate)*, with a lovely garden, a pool and a children's playground, is 900 m from the beach in a wood. Information: *68, Rue de la Plage | tel. 05 56 09 86 61 | www.soulac.com*

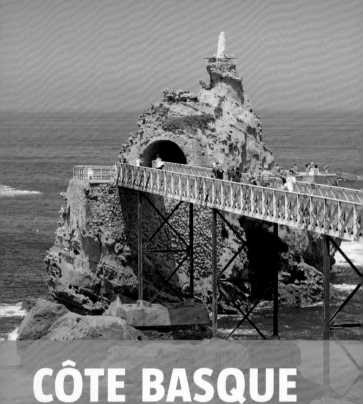

CÔTE BASQUE

The landscape changes just short of Biarritz. The wide sandy beaches of *les Landes* are replaced by the rugged Basque coast that extends for 30km (19mi) on the French side.

And it becomes more glamourous too. The wealthy have been coming to Biarritz since time immemorial. Originally it was European aristocrats, nowadays it is film stars and the *nouveau riche*. And Saint-Jean-de-Luz has less to do with seaside resorts so familiar further up the Atlantic coast and more with elegant holiday destinations on the Mediterranean.

Many signs are in two languages – French and *Euskara* (Basque) – with a noticeable number of 'x's 'k's suddenly appearing. But unlike on the Spanish side, there is no separatist movement in the French part of the Basque Country. The only wish that is expressed from time to time is to have a département of their own. The Basque language that was once in danger of becoming extinct, is now being carefully nurtured.

BIARRITZ

MAP INSIDE BACK COVER
(134 B5) (*ɰ C16*) Hydrangeas in bloom, steep alleyways, lovely shops and

Photo: Rocher de la Vierge in Biarritz

Elegant seaside towns on a rugged coastline:
exclusive resorts, picturesque fishing villages
and the Pyrenees waiting to be explored

views everywhere of the sea: the resort and surfer eldorado (pop. 26,000) is a jewel on the Atlantic Coast.

Biarritz, where the sun shines on the Grande Plage 2000 hours a year, has given its glory-of-old a fresh glamourous look. Napoleon III and his empress Eugénie – who fell in love with the fishing port long before she got married – made it fashionable. The royal household ac-companied them *en vacances* and soon kings and tzars dropped by, and Biarritz became a meeting place for high society. Apart from thalassotherapy, golf and surf-ing, tourist attractions include pelota matches and Basque competitions of strength.

La grande dame of seaside resorts is mod-est in size, but gets pretty crowded in the high season. Despite this, parking (at a

How do you get from the Atlantic to Asia in 5 minutes? Just visit the Musée Asiatica

charge) in the centre is still relatively easy. The Old Town is small; the museums, market hall, beaches and Old Port can all be reached on foot.

SIGHTSEEING

CHAPELLE IMPÉRIALE
The imperial chapel was built for Empress Eugénie in 1864 in the Romanesque and Byzantine style with Moorish elements. *Rue Pellot | June–Sept Thu and Sat, April/ May and Oct Sat 2.30pm–6pm, March and Nov/Dec Sat 2.30pm–5pm*

CITÉ DE L'OCÉAN ET DU SURF
This hands-on museum, designed by the New York architect Steven Holl in the shape of a wave, focuses on all aspects of marine research and protection. How the oceans were created and why man is dependent on them, for example, are explained in an informative and entertaining way. The section devoted to the

secrets and sagas of the sea is particularly thrilling – such as the notorious Bermuda Triange and the Flood in the Bible. *1, Avenue de la Plage | July/Aug daily 10am–11pm, April–June and Sept/Oct 10am–7pm, Nov– March 10am–6pm | www.citedelocean.com*

INSIDER TIP MUSÉE ASIATICA
With more than 1000 exhibits from India, Tibet, Nepal and China, this is one of the most important museums of Asian art in Europe. *1, Rue Guy Petit | July/Aug daily 10.30–6pm, Sept–June 2pm–6pm | www. museeasiatica.com*

MUSÉE HISTORIQUE DE BIARRITZ
The history of the town's beginnings and its heyday presented in the former Anglican church. *Rue Broquedis | Tue–Sat 10am–1pm and 2.30pm–6.30pm*

MUSÉE DE LA MER AQUARIUM ★
The museum has recently been revamped and is now twice the size – and a fascinat-

ing experience not only for families. The main focal points are the marine worlds in the Bay of Biscay and the Caribbean that are presented in 12 aquariums and an 11m (36ft)-long lagoon and are home to more than 300 species. A tour leads on to Cape Horn and the Pacific where sharks and rays can be seen. Seal feeding is at 10.30am and 5pm and is very popular among younger visitors. *Esplanade du Rocher de la Vierge | July/Aug daily 9.30am–midnight, April–June and Sept/Oct 9.30am–8pm, Nov–March 9.30am–7pm | www.museedelamer.com*

PHARE SAINT-MARTIN ☆
Built in 1834, the 73m (240ft)-high white lighthouse is situated on Mont Saint-Martin that divides the sandy beaches of *les Landes* from the rocky Basque coastline. After climbing the 248 steps, you will be rewarded with a superb view all the way to Spain. *July/Aug daily 10am–1.30pm and 2pm–7pm, May/June and Sept 2pm–6pm, Oct–April Sat/Sun, during school holidays daily 2pm–5pm*

PLANÈTE MUSÉE DU CHOCOLAT
The history and art of chocolate-making. *14, Avenue Beaurivage | July/Aug daily 10am–6.30pm, Sept–June Mon–Sat 10am–12.30pm and 2.30pm–6.30pm | www.planetemuseeduchocolat.com*

ROCHER DE LA VIERGE ☆
The iron bridge that links the wave-lashed rock with the mainland, is reputed to have been built by Gustave Eiffel. The statue of the Virgin Mary has been perched on the rock since 1865.

FOOD & DRINK

CHEZ ALBERT
Fish and seafood on the old fishing harbour. *Closed Wed except in July/Aug | Port des Pêcheurs | tel. 05 59 24 43 84 | www.chezalbert.fr | Moderate*

LE BALEAK
Traditional Basque cuisine with imaginative fish specialities is served in a friendly, brightly-lit restaurant near the market. *Closed Sun/Mon except in July/Aug | 8, Rue du Centre | tel. 05 59 24 58 57 | www.baleak.fr | Moderate*

MARCO POLO HIGHLIGHTS

★ **The Grande Plage in Biarritz**
The main beach in Biarritz is one of the most elegant and beautiful in Europe → **p. 89**

★ **Hotel du Palais in Biarritz**
If this legendary hotel is too hard at the purse strings, at least treat yourself to an *apértif* – the glamourous flair comes free of charge → **p. 89**

★ **Hossegor**
This surfing eldorado is one of the most beautiful beaches on the Atlantic Coast → **p. 91**

★ **Saint-Jean-de-Luz**
Let yourself be taken in by the magical atmosphere of this romantic little town → **p. 92**

★ **Musée de la Mer Aquarium in Biarritz**
The interactive aquarium will turn everyone into a hobby marine biologist → **p. 86**

★ **Corniche Basque**
A simply fantastic coast road → **p. 95**

Spain is really not far away: *tapas* in Bar Jean near the market in Biarritz

LE BISTROT DE L'HUÎTRE

Lovely small oyster and seafood restaurant 200m from the Grande Plage. Very good *foie gras. Daily | 29, Boulevard du Général de Gaulle | tel. 05 59 22 31 32 | Moderate*

INSIDER TIP BAR JEAN

Right next to the market halls; breakfast and *tapas*; ideal for watching the world go by. *Daily | 5, Rue des Halles | tel. 05 59 24 80 38 | www.barjean-biarritz.com | Budget*

INSIDER TIP JERÔME 🌀

From outside, this post-modern ice cream parlour looks like a cookery studio. The ice cream itself, made without any colouring or preservatives, comes in flavours such as 'Neige de Sahara' (with lemon and orange petals) and 'Salty Dog' (pink grapefruit, vodka and herbs) which prove that making good ice cream is an art. *8, Avenue de Verdun*

LA PLANCHA D'ILBARITZ

Situated a little to the south in Bidart. This is the place to meet for a sundowner. *Closed Wed | Avenue du Lac/Plage d'Ilbaritz | tel. 05 59 23 44 95 | Budget*

SISSINOU

The menu has just 5 fish and meat dishes and, from the outside, Sissinou is easy to miss. Inside, however, you will be able to enjoy exceptionally creative food. *Closed Sun/Mon except in Aug | 5, Avenue Maréchal Foch | tel. 05 59 22 51 50 | Expensive*

SHOPPING

The range of shops in Biarritz is beguiling. A market is held every morning in two halls (fish, groceries), both with loud piped music. Outside there are stands with clothes. Cheerful Basque table linen, not only in traditional striped patterns, e.g. at *Euskal Linge (14, Rue Mazagran).*

Delicious cheese can be found at *Mille et un Fromage (8, Avenue Victor Hugo)*. Chocolate, pralinés and all sorts of other yummy things are made by *Chocolatier Henriet (Place Clemenceau)*. The *factory (3, Avenue De Bassilour | tel. 05 59 47 58 58)*, in Bidart, can be visited by prior appointment.

SPORTS & BEACHES

The largest and most beautiful beach is the ★ *Grande Plage*, that runs from the Hotel du Palais to Bellevue. The sea here however is anything but tame – which makes is excellent for surfing. Surfing is forbidden on *Plage Miramar* due to the strong currents. Surfers love *La Côte des Basques* beach. *Le Port Vieux* is a relatively small but sheltered beach and is suitable for swimming. But that's what a lot of dogs think too. *Marbella* and *Milade* beaches – that are also surfers' territory – are more glamourous.

Surfing is as much a part of Biarritz as salt is to the sea. Several schools offer courses. There are 10 golf courses in and around Biarritz. The golf pass provides access to 5 courses; information from Golf Biarritz Le Phare.

Riders head for *Club Hippique de Biarritz (Allée Gabrielle Dorziat | tel. 05 59 23 52 33 | www.biarritzcheval.com)*. 3 diving schools are located in the Port des Pêcheurs; a heated seawater pool for cooler weather can be found in the casino building. Anyone wanting to try their hand at pelota shoud contact *Biarritz Athlétic Club (Parc des Sports d'Aguiléra | tel. 05 59 23 91 09 | www.cesta-punta.com)*.

ENTERTAINMENT

Bar Royalty (Place Clemenceau) has a lovely terrace, popular by a youngish crowd. The disco *Le BL* and the lounge bar

Carré Coast (www.lecarrecoast.com) are part of the Art Déco *casino* on the promenade. Hip clubs include *Le Copa (24, Avenue Édouard VIII)*, *Le Caveau (4, Rue Gambetta | www.lecaveau-biarritz.com)*, *Ibiza (Grande Plage | www.ibiza-biarritz.com)* and *Blue Cargo (Avenue Ilbaritz)*.

WHERE TO STAY

ALCYON

Small hotel with a pretty and cheerful breakfast room. *15 rooms | 8, Rue Maison Suisse | tel. 05 59 22 64 60 | www.hotel-alcyon-biarritz.com | Moderate*

HOTEL ANJOU

Simply furnished but friendly and well-looked-after hotel 300m from the beach. Some rooms have balconies and/or a view of the sea. *30 rooms | 18, Rue Gambetta | tel. 05 59 24 00 93 | www.hotel-anjou.fr | Budget–Moderate*

LE CARITZ ⚓

This small hotel is on the beach at the old harbour. Basque dishes are served in the restaurant or on the large terrace in nice weather. *10 rooms, 2 suites | Plage du Port Vieux | tel. 05 59 24 41 84 | www.lecaritz.com | Expensive*

HÔTEL PALACITO

Very central location 200m from the beach. Completely renovated in 2011, the hotel is decorated in blues and whites. The rooms are modern and stylishly furnished. The hotel has its own café. *24 rooms | 1, Rue Gambetta | tel. 05 59 24 04 89 | www.palacito.fr | Expensive*

HOTEL DU PALAIS ★

Stay in imperial luxury. The hotel, one of the 'Leading Hotels of the World', was once the summer residence of Napoleon III and Empress Eugénie and is correspondingly magnificent. Pool, spa and 3 restaurants. *154 rooms | 1, Avenue de l'Impératrice | tel. 05 59 41 64 00 | www. hotel-du-palais.com | Expensive*

private car park. Some of the 🌿 rooms on the 3rd floor have a view of the sea. *20 rooms | 20, Avenue Carnot | tel. 05 59 24 20 39 | www.saint-julien-biarritz.com | Expensive*

INFORMATION

Square d'Ixelles | tel. 05 59 22 37 10 | www. biarritz.fr

WHERE TO GO

BAYONNE (134 B5) (*𝄞 C16*)

The port of Bayonne (pop. 43,000) on the lower Adour was a free trading area from 1784 onwards and an important hub in dealings with the Antilles, Spain and Holland. The arms business also helped the town 10km (6mi) east of Biarritz to riches – it was here that the bayonet was invented and sold in huge numbers around the globe.

The beautiful Old Town is well worth seeing as are the Gothic *Cathedrale Sainte-Marie (Place Pasteur | Mon–Sat 10am–11.45am and 3pm–5.45pm, Sun 3.30pm–6pm)* and the ● INSIDER TIP▶ Musée Basque *(37, Quai des Corsaires | July/Aug Fri–Wed 10am–6.30pm, Thu 10am–8.30pm, April– June and Sept Tue–Sun 10am–6.30pm, Oct–March 10am–6pm | www.musee-basque.com)* that is devoted to the Basque culture. *Musée Bonnat (5, Rue Jacques Laffitte | July/Aug Fri–Wed 10am–6.30pm, Thu 10am–9.30pm, May/June and Sept/ Oct Wed–Mon 10am–6.30pm, Nov–April Wed–Mon 10am–12.30pm and 2pm–6pm | www.musee-bonnat.com)* with works by Goya, Rubens, Degas and El Greco is equally rewarding.

Bayonne's Old Town, with its proud patricians' houses and Basque half-timbering, is an attractive and lively place to stroll around and go shopping. A lot of *chocolatiers* can be found here too, e.g. *Atelier*

The towers of Sainte-Marie's cathedral dominate the Old Town of Bayonne

HÔTEL SAINT JULIEN

Lovely 19th-century hotel stylishly furnished in pastel shades. Its small garden is an oasis of peace and quiet in the heart of Biarritz. Guests have free use of the

du Chocolat (7, Allée de Gibéléou | www. atelierduchocolat.fr) and several other tempting addresses on *Rue Port-Neuf,* ever since cocoa was unloaded in the port here in the 17th century.

The former professional pelota player Jean-Pierre Marmouyet has decorated his restaurant *Le Chistera (closed on Mon, and Tue/Wed evenings out of season | 42, Rue Port-Neuf | tel. 05 59 59 25 93 | www. lechistera.com | Budget)* with all sorts of sports paraphernalia, and serves down-to-earth Basque fare at very reasonable prices. The nicest place to sit is outside under the 200-year-old arcades. The food served in the Michelin Star restaurant *Auberge du Cheval Blanc (closed Sat lunch-time, Sun evening and Mon | 68, Rue Bourgneuf | tel. 05 59 59 01 33 | www. cheval-blanc-bayonne.com | Expensive)* is ambitious and with a regional touch. Try the duck *confit!* Information: *Place des Basques | tel. 08 20 42 64 64 | www. bayonne-tourisme.com*

CAPBRETON (134 B4) (*ʘ C15*)

The bathing resort, fishing harbour and marina (pop. 4800), with a wide range of facilities for watersports enthusiasts, 19

tennis courts and a casino, is 25km (15½mi) north of Biarritz. *Hôtel Porto Rico (20 rooms | 4, Rue de Madrid | tel. 05 58 41 38 63 | www.hotelportorico.fr | Budget)* is a welcoming place to stay, furnished in a sleek contemporary style, just 50m from the beach and port with a garden and private car park. Information: *Avenue du Président Pompidou | tel. 05 58 72 12 11 | www.capbreton-tourisme.com*

DAX (134 C4) (*ʘ D15*)

Even the Romans came here to take the waters. France's oldest spa (pop. 20,000) is a good 50km (30mi) northeast of Biarritz. Dax is still famous for its thermal springs and several Roman remains can be seen too. Information: *11, Cours Foch | tel. 05 58 56 86 86 | www.dax-tourisme.com*

HOSSEGOR ★
(134 B4) (*ʘ C15*)

Hossegor is only separated from Capbreton to the south by a tributary of the Adour. Before it reaches its mouth the river widens to form Lac d'Hossegor where celebrities and the well-off settled in the 1920s and '30s around the shore. Today it has become INSIDER TIP one of the top addresses in the

FORCE BASQUE

The types of sports that the Basques have kept alive since time immemorial are archaic indeed – tug-of-war *(soka-tira),* wood chopping *(aizkolariak),* turning a heavy ox-cart on its own axis *(orga joko)* and stone-lifting *(harri altxatzea)* – and that really does mean lifting: the stones weigh several hundred kilograms. What had its origins in the everyday needs of a farming community now takes

the form of the *Force Basque,* competitions with strict rules that are battled out between teams from Basque villages. The best known festival is held in Saint-Palais in August. The traditional Basque ball game – pelota, a kind of Basque version of fives or squash that two teams play against a *fronton,* a high wall – can also be played by those who are not bodybuilders!

world for surfers. The drop in the seabed beyond the sandbanks is deep, allowing particularly big waves to form. Golf, wind-surfing, tennis and cycling are popular pastimes here as well as surfing. Anybody wanting to improve their surfing should head for ● *École de Surf Aloha (900, Route de la Tuilerie | tel. 06 99 55 01 96 | www. aloha-ecoledesurf.com)*.

The lakeside hotel *Las Hortensias du Lac (18 rooms | 1578, Avenue du Tour du Lac | tel. 05 58 43 99 00 | www.hortensias-du-lac.com | Expensive)*, exudes a country-house atmosphere. Readers of Armistead Maupin's 'Tales of the City' series of novels on the other hand will enjoy the hotel *Barbary Lane (18 rooms | 156, Avenue de la Côte d'Argent | tel. 05 58 43 46 00 | www.barbary-lane.com | Moderate)* that is INSIDER TIP based on the main location in these works. *Hôtel 202 (22 rooms | 202, Avenue du Golf | tel. 05 58 43 22 02 | www. hotel202.fr | Expensive)* in the centre of Hossegor is elegant and stylish and close to the golf club in Soorts. Information: *Place des Halles | tel. 05 58 41 79 00 | www. hossegor.fr*

ONDRES-PLAGE

(134 B4) (*M C16*)

The 2km (1¼mi)-long sandy beach makes Ondres-Plage an attractive resort. The little spa town (pop. 4200) comes under the administration of the Landes – like Capbreton and Hossegor – and not the Basque Country. However, the culture here is undoubtedly Basque as shown, for example, in the locals' love of pelota. Pine forestry is no longer the most important industry but tourism instead. *Le Lodge (25 rooms | 1180, Avenue du 11 Novembre 1918 | tel. 05 59 45 27 02 | www.hotel-le-lodge.com | Moderate)* is a quietly situated hotel with friendly service and a small pool where breakfast is served on the terrace. Information: *1750, Avenue du 11 Novembre 1918 | tel. 05 59 45 19 19 | www.seignanx-tourisme.com*

SAINT-JEAN-DE-LUZ

(134 B5) (*M C16*) ★ **The particularly beautiful fishing port and resort of Saint-Jean-de-Luz lies 10km (6mi) from the Spanish border.**

The legacy of this former whaling village is still alive today, with at least one person is almost every local family working as a fisherman. The Old Town is tucked away behind the harbour, beyond that is the beach that is protected from the fierce Atlantic by sea walls. The highest waves in the Atlantic have been recorded here just 2km (1¼mi) from the coast. Surfers are taken out to the waves on jet skis or even by helicopter.

In 1660, world history was written in Saint-Jean-de-Luz when the Sun King, Louis XIV, married the Spanish Infanta Maria Theresia – an alliance that sealed peace between the two countries after 24 years of war and ensured France's position of supremacy in Europe. Today, the town has almost joined up with *Ciboure* (pop. 6000) on the left bank of the River Nivelle.

SIGHTSEEING

PORT

Saint-Jean-de-Luz has always been a wealthy place. The houses on the port were built by prosperous shipowners and their façades are a colourful mixture of styles that testify to the owners cosmopolitan history. Almost every house has a look-out tower with a view of the harbour from which enemies as well as ships returning home could be spotted.

MAISON LOUIS XIV

The monarch spent 40 days in this house built in 1643 in preparation for his wedding. Furniture from the period and an exhibition bring this legendary union and the history of the town to life. *Place Louis XIV | June and Sept/Oct guided tours daily 11am, 3pm, 4pm and 5pm, July/Aug 10.30am–12.30pm and 2.30pm–6.30pm*

PLACE LOUIS XIV

This square exudes the charm of the south with its cafés, bars and music pavilion in the middle. Artists set up their easels in pleted for the Sun King's wedding and replaced the medieval church that had become too small. The exterior is plain and simple whereas, inside, the gold-plated retable is a demonstration of Saint-Jean-de-Luz's wealth.

FOOD & DRINK

L'ALCALDE

Basque dishes and seafood. *Parrilladas,* platters of grilled fish, are a speciality. *Closed Sun evening and Mon Nov–April |*

Maison Louis XIV: the bed in which the imperial couple spent their first night

the shade of the plane trees while pastis is sipped in the bars round about. This is also where you'll find the house where the Sun King resided.

SAINT-JEAN-BAPTISTE

The 17th-century church with the short, octagonal (look-out) tower was com-

22, Rue de la République | tel. 05 59 26 89 44 | www.restaurant-alcalde.com | Moderate

LE DAUPHIN

Fish and seafood with a view of the ocean in a rustic setting. *Daily | 39, Place de la Pergola | tel. 05 59 26 00 69 | www.restaurantledauphin.com | Budget*

LE KAIKU

Very good fish and lamb dishes in the oldest building in the town. *Closed Mon | 17, Rue de la République | tel. 05 59 26 13 20 | Moderate*

SHOPPING

A market is held every morning in the ● indoor market, with local products also available on Tue, Fri and Sat outside. Most boutiques are concentrated on the *Rue Gambetta.* Local materials in typically Basque coloured stripes are stocked by *Maison Charles Larre (Place Louis XIV | www.maisoncharleslarre.com).*

Delicious almond macaroons that were reputedly savoured at the Sun King's wedding are still made to the same recipe at INSIDER TIP *Maison Adam (6, Rue de la République | www.macarons-adam.com).* Sample the chillies dunked in chocolate at the same time!

LOW BUDGET

▶ Hossegor has a number of outlet stores for surfing accessories, as befits a surfers' mecca. Bargains can also be found, for example, in the outlets *Billabong (128, Avenue des Sabotiers | July/Aug Mon–Sat 10am–8pm, otherwise 10am–1pm and 3pm–7pm)* and *Quiksilver (114, Rue des Vanniers | Tue–Sat 9.30am–12.30pm and 2pm–6pm).*

▶ If you visit the *Musée Basque* in Bayonne in July and August on a Wed evening after 6.30pm it won't cost you a penny!

SPORTS & ACTIVITIES

All kinds of watersports from jet skiing to surfing rank top in Saint-Jean-de-Luz. Sailing, diving and waterskiing can be learnt in neighbouring Ciboure. Bicycles can be rented at the station. Golf players head for *Golf de Chantaco (Route d'Ascain | tel. 05 59 26 14 22 | www.chantaco.com).* There is an indoor swimming pool in *Route d'Ascain.* Pelota can be played in *Trinquet Anderenia (Quartier Ametzague | tel. 05 59 26 12 12).* A 2-hour introductory course *(Mon and Thu, July/Aug also Tue 10am)* can be booked through the tourist information office. Thalassotherapy: ● *Hélianthal | Place Maurice Ravel | tel. 05 59 51 51 51 | www.helianthal.fr*

ENTERTAINMENT

Bets are placed in the elegant *casino (Place Maurice Ravel).* A popular club is *Mata Hari (Avenue André Ithurralde).* Many night owls go clubbing in Biarritz.

WHERE TO STAY

INSIDER TIP LES ALMADIES

Small, beautifully furnished hotel near the port and the beach. Lovely wooden terrace for a sundowner. *7 rooms | 58, Rue Gambetta | tel. 05 59 85 34 48 | www.hotel-les-almadies.com | Expensive*

OHARTZIA

Pretty hotel with simple rooms in the town centre. The shady flower garden is bliss on hot days. *17 rooms | 28, Rue Garat | tel. 05 59 26 00 06 | www.hotel-ohartzia.com | Moderate*

INFORMATION

20, Boulevard Victor Hugo | tel. 05 59 26 03 16 | www.saint-jean-de-luz.com

Climbing up from the Côte Basque into the Pyrenean mountains

WHERE TO GO

CORNICHE BASQUE ★
(134 A–B5) (*B–C16*)

The coastal road, the Route de la Corniche (D 912), starts to the southwest of Saint-Jean-de-Luz and runs along the rugged Basque coastline towards the Spanish border. Apart from the wonderful views over the Atlantic, you can also marvel at the largely unspoilt coastal scenery.

HENDAYE-PLAGE
(134 A5) (*B16*)

12km (7½mi) to the west of Saint-Jean-de-Luz, just before the Spanish border, is Hendaye-Plage (pop. 11,000), a lively albeit not particularly elegant bathing resort. Its plus points include the wide almost 3km (2mi)-long beach with relatively gentle waves and several beautiful old villas set in lovely gardens. Information: *67, Boulevard de la Mer | tel. 05 59 20 00 34 | www.hendaye-tourisme.fr*

SARE AND LA RHUNE
(134 B5) (*C16–17*)

Sare (pop. 2200) lies 14km (9mi) to the south. The *Grottes de Sare (April–June and Sept daily 10am–6pm, July/Aug 10am–7pm, Oct 10am–5pm, Nov–March 2pm–5pm | www.grottesdesare.fr)*, caves that were first inhabited 45,000 years ago, are remarkable. Their history is presented in a *son et lumière* show.

Nearby, on the Pass Saint-Ignace, is the station for the *Petit Train de la Rhune*. This historic rack-and-pinion railway climbs up the 900m (2953ft)-high Pyrenean mountain, the summit of which is on Spanish territory. *April–Sept daily, Oct Tue/Wed and Fri–Sun 9.30am, 11.30am, 2pm and 4pm, July/Aug every 35 mins. | 14 euros, in July/Aug 17 euros | www.rhune.com*

TRIPS & TOURS

The tours are marked in green in the road atlas, the pull-out map and on the back cover

1 WINE TASTING IN GRAVES, SAUTERNES AND ENTRE-DEUX-MERS

So you're tired of heady claret? Then how about trying your luck along the Graves and Entre-Deux-Mers route? The dry white wines originating from Pessac-Léognan and the outstanding sweet wines from Barsac and Sauternes are the sole classified whites in this region. Bordeaux is the starting point of this 180km (112mi) tour through the Graves countryside that stretches to the south of Bordeaux as far as Langon on the left bank of the Garonne, and the Entre-Deux-Mers area – that does not lie between two seas but between the rivers Garonne and Dordogne. Plan 3 days to be able to look around, sample the wine and enjoy the area without being rushed. Those in a hurry can complete the tour with a few stops in 2 days.

The Route des Grands Crus Classés starts not far from Bordeaux → p. 71 in the Pessac-Léognan wine growing area. Leave the city centre and head for Pessac, passing through idyllic countryside to Léognan and continue towards Martillac on the D109. You should plan a stop at La Brède to visit the moated castle → p. 76 where the famous political thinker Baron de Montesquieu lived.

Photo: The Pyrenees in the Basque Country

Vineyards, forests, water and pretty villages:
five tours in Bordelais, the Pyrenees, the Loire
estuary, Arcachon Bay and Mimizan

From here, take the N113 through the Graves wine growing area where aromatic red and elegant dry wines are produced as well as mellow whites. The Belvédère water tower designed by Le Corbusier can be marvelled at in **Podensac**. This is also the home of the *apéritif* Lillet, a mixture of wine and macerated liqueur. The distillery and cellar are open to the public *(Maison de Lillet | RN113 | mid June–mid Sept daily 10am–6pm | www.lillet.com)*. A lovely place to stay is **Château du Broustaret** *(5 rooms | 1, Truilley | tel. 05 56 62 96 97 | www.broustaret.net | Budget)*, a 19th-century country house in a parkland setting in **Rions**. To get there, cross to the right bank of the river after Podensac.

The next day – back on the left bank of the Garonne again – follow the N113 towards Cérons, Barsac and **Sauternes**, the world-famous wine growing areas for dessert wines that are, by the way, a perfect accompaniment to *foie gras* just as much as to flavour some cheeses. Making them is very labour intensive as the yield from the dry grape harvest is so low that only about one glassful can be gleaned from

the south, to Saint-Martin-de-Lerm, you can stay overnight in the converted stables on the tithe farm INSIDERTIP *La Lézardière (5 rooms | 9, Boimier | tel. 05 56 71 30 12 | lalezardiere.free.fr | Budget)* which dates from the 17th century and has a lovely garden and pool.

The Roman bridge in Ascain across the Nivelle which is popular for rafting

each vine – which is later reflected in the price. Cross the Garonne again near Langon. The 14th-century defensive walls in Saint-Macaire just beyond Langon and Saint-Sauveur church are well worth seeing.

Now you leave the Graves region heading northeast on the D672 towards Sainte-Foy-La-Grande and reach Entre-Deux-Mers, the most extensive wine growing area in Bordelais. If you make a short detour to

You return to Bordeaux on the D936 via Saint-Michel-de-Montaigne, the home of the famous essayist, and Castillon-la-Bataille.

2 THE PYRENEES IN THE BASQUE COUNTRY

It is well worth taking some time to explore the Basque Country inland from the sea with its well

kept villages of whitewashed and ruddy coloured half-timbered houses, set among the green foothills of the Pyrenees. The route goes from Saint-Jean-de-Luz through picturesque Basque villages to Cambo-les-Bains and Saint-Jean-Pied-de-Port. This tour is approx. 160km (100mi) long and passes through mountainous scenery. Take your time to explore the wonderful countryside on foot as well. In 2–3 days you'll be able to see a lot.

The village of Ascain on the Nivelle, about 6km (4mi) from the coast, is reached on the D4. The river here is fast flowing – perfect for rafting – and is crossed by a restored Roman bridge. The medieval church is well worth a visit. Stay on the D4 past Sare → p. 95 until you reach Ainhoa that has been named one of the prettiest villages in France. It was founded in the 12th century as a stopping place for pilgrims on the Way of St James. The *fronton*, the pelota court, is just as much part of the Basque idyll as the 5-storey bell tower and the chapel Notre-Dame d'Aranzazu with its gilded wooden sculptures. The restaurant Itthuria *(closed Thu lunchtime and Wed Sept–June | Place du Fronton | tel. 05 59 29 92 11 | www.itthuria.com | Moderate–Expensive)* provides Basque cuisine of a high standard in a restored pilgrims' resting house. It also has 27 lovely bedrooms.

Espelette, on the D20, is one of the most photographed villages in the region on account of the red peppers that are hung on house walls to dry in the autumn. One place to stay is the traditional Basque *Hotel Euzkadi (27 rooms | 285, Karrika Nagusia | tel. 05 59 93 91 88 | www.hotel-restaurant-euzkadi.com | Budget)* with its own restaurant *(closed Mon/Tue)*.

Cambo-les-Bains, just a few miles beyond Espelette, is a traditional spa with a lower and upper town. A visit to the magnificent Villa Arnaga *(Route du Docteur Camino |* July/Aug daily 10am–7pm, April–June and Sept–mid Oct 9.30am–12.30pm and 2.30pm–6pm, at other times by prior appointment: tel. 05 59 29 83 92 | www.arnaga.com) with its wonderful library, many paintings and formal gardens, is a must.

A further 30km (19mi) up into the Pyrenees along the D918, you come to Saint-Jean-Pied-de-Port, a beautiful little town 8km (5mi) from the Spanish border that is much visited in the summer. Apart from the massive fortified walls, its citadel is a reminder of the permanent threat the town faced in the olden days being so close to the border. Les Pyrénées *(closed Mon evening | 14 rooms | 19, Place du Général de Gaulle | tel. 05 47 20 80 35 | www.hotel-les-pyrenees.com | Expensive)* is a stylish hotel with a gourmet restaurant (Basque cuisine) and a pool.

From Saint-Jean follow the Route Impériale des Cimes (D22) towards the coast. Just before Hasparren turn right to the Grottes d'Isturitz et d'Oxocelhaya *(July/Aug daily 10am–1pm and 2pm–6pm, guided tours daily in June and Sept at 11am, noon, 2pm and 5pm, March–May and Oct/Nov daily 2pm–5pm | www.grottes-isturitz.com)*. There are stalactites in Oxocelhaya and prehistoric rock engravings in Isturitz. From here, it is 30km (19mi) to Bayonne → p. 90 and another 20 km (12½mi) to Saint-Jean-de-Luz.

 CULTURE, COUNTRYSIDE AND INDUSTRY IN THE LOIRE ESTUARY

    The whole of the Loire estuary can be explored by bike. Those who don't want to go too far from the coast but still want to see something of the countryside inland should go on a 50km (31mi) cycle tour from Nantes that takes in the history of the region.

This route is perfect for a day's outing. If you just cycle along the canal, you can cover the flat 15km (9½mi) is less than 2 hours.

The route starts at the station in Nantes → p. 38. The cycle path follows the north bank of the Loire to start with, heading westwards, passing the old port and Chantenay. In Couëron, take the *bac,* the free ferry, across the Loire to Le Pellerin on the south bank. Keep on the left bank as far as the Canal de la Martinière. This waterway was dug out in the 19th century so that larger ships could reach Nantes and was opened in 1892. Due to the sandbanks, the Loire was frequently impassable for bigger ships between Paimbœuf and Le Pellerin. However, at the beginning of the 20th century, the canal was abandoned. It is now used to regulate the water in the marshlands and the surrounding area and has become part of a particularly idyllic stretch of unspoilt countryside.

After a gentle 10km (6mi) ride along the canal you reach Paimbœuf, where a section of the aire cultural project can be seen. This gradually came into being between 2007–12, aimed at injecting new impulses into this former industrial area. There are now numerous art installations throughout the Loire estuary between Nantes and Saint-Nazaire. Le Jardin Étoilé, a work of art by Kinya Maruyama that you could walk around, was however damaged by Cyclone Xynthia in winter 2010, followed by a fire. Restoration is in progress.

If you don't want to go back the same way, carry on a further 12km (7½mi) to beyond Saint-Brévin-les-Pins. From here you can take your bike on bus (line 17) (to reserve space for free bike transport *tel. 02 40 21 50 87*) and reach Saint-Nazaire in 20 mins. Another alternative is to keep on the bike path for another 13km (8mi) and

cross the spectacular bridge over the Loire estuary to Saint-Nazaire. Heavy traffic and strong winds however can make this variation less attractive. Trains from Saint-Nazaire to Nantes take 40 mins.; bikes can be taken on local trains free of charge. Information about the whole cycle path along the Loire can be found under *www.cycling-loire.com*; the aire cultural project under *www.aire.info*.

4 SANDBANKS AND SALT MARSHES: AROUND ARCACHON BAY

This 64km (40km)-long day-trip near the coast around the Bassin d'Arcachon offers lots of variety and wonderful panoramic views. The route is ideal for energetic cyclists.

Start at the spur of Cap Ferret → p. 68 from where you have a good view of Arguin sandbank. If you're feeling fit climb the 52m (170ft)-high lighthouse ☀ Phare du Cap Ferret, and soak up the spectacular view as far as the Dune du Pilat.

Otherwise take the D106 to the north towards Le Grand-Piquey, passing the oyster beds and with a view across to Île-aux-Oiseaux in Arcachon Bay. The next stop is Arès at the northern end of the bay. The route crosses saltmarshes before reaching the lively resorts Andernos-les-Bains and Lanton where you can enjoy a break in one of the cafés before pressing on to Audenge. From here, things are more peaceful. The sound of gulls and numerous other birds can be heard south of Lanton as you approach the Parc Ornithologique du Teich *(July/Aug daily 10am–8pm, mid April–June and 1st half of Sept 10am–7pm mid Sept–mid April 10am–6pm | www.parc-ornithologique-du-teich.com)*, which is also accessible to cyclists.

In Gujan-Mestras it becomes more urban again. In the self-proclaimed oyster farm ing capital – more than half the oysters grown in the bay come from here – you can inform yourself about all aspects of oyster cultivation in the **Maison de l'Huître** *(June–Aug daily, Sept–May Mon–Sat 10am–12.30pm and 2.30pm–6pm | Port de Larros | www.maisondelhuitre.fr)*. If you want to sample the seafood, try the adjoining restaurant **Les Pavois** *(closed Mon/Tue except in July/Aug | 113, Port de Larros | tel. 05 56 66 38 71 | www.restaurant-lespavois.com | Budget)*.

The final stretch is from Gujan to **Arcachon → p. 65.** From here, you can use the boat service to return to Cap Ferret. Line 1 takes you back to where you started, leaving from Jetée Thiers, in 30 mins *(July/Aug daily 9am–8pm on the hour, April–June and Sept/Oct at 9am, 11am, noon, 2pm, 4pm and 5.30pm | www.bateliers-arcachon.com)*.

5 THE FRAGRANT FORESTS INLAND FROM MIMIZAN

This gentle cycle tour or hike on the Côte d'Argent covers 17km (10½mi) and goes from Mimizan-Plage along the Courant to the Étang d'Aureilhan, Saint-Paul-en-Born and on to Pontenx-les-Forges.

The starting point is the Boulevard de l'Atlantique in **Mimizan-Plage → p. 77.** The route follows the D626 from the coast through a quiet residential area with a number of beautifully restored houses before heading eastwards through the forest. You then cross the D87 onto the Avenue du Lac that leads to the Étang d'Aureilhan. Up as far as Aureilhan the cycle path runs along the road beside the river.

There is a nice picnic site in **Aureilhan** on the shore of the delightful lake. After a short break take the Route du Bourg and

carry on along the D626 to **Saint-Paul-en-Born.** Keep on the D626 for another 2.5km (1½mi) before reaching **Pontenx-les-Forges** along the Chemin de Pécam and Avenue de Mimizan. Hikers can take

The Parc du Teich: clattering sounds don't necessarily come from your bike

the bus (line 13) from here back to Mimizan-Plage. Of course, you can do this in reverse, first taking the bus to Pontenx and then hiking to the coast.

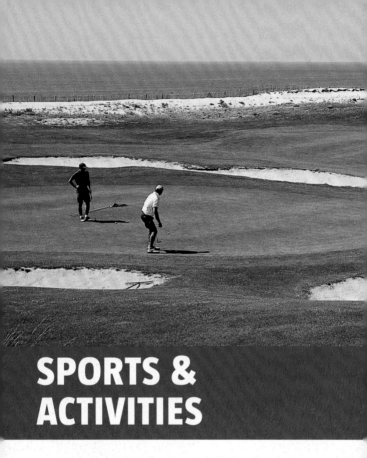

SPORTS & ACTIVITIES

You certainly won't get bored here! Sport is just as much part of the French Atlantic Coast's tourist capital as its wide beaches. An excellent infrastructure for all forms of watersport awaits you on the inland lakes and the Côte d'Argent. On top of this, there is a well established network of cycle paths and bridleways and masses of golf courses.

CANOE & KAYAK TRIPS

Canoe and kayak trips are available on the sea, rivers and lakes. The quality seal of approval 'Point Canoë Nature' awarded by the *Fédération Française de Canoë Kayak (www.ffck.org, www.ffcanoe.asso.fr)* is an indication of a private company's high standards. The Bassin d'Arcachon, the Lac d'Hourtin et de Carcans, the Lac de Lacanau and the Lac de Cazaux et de Sanguinet are ideal for both canoe and kayak trips.

CYCLING

The generally flat Atlantic coast is perfect for cycle tours. Over the past few years bike touring facilities have been expanded greatly in southwest France. There are around 2000km (1250mi) of cycle paths between Biscarrosse and Ondres near Capbreton alone and 1000km (620mi) in the Vendée with more than 70 way

Photo: Golf course in Moliets on the Côte d'Argent

With plenty of wind and waves the only thing to stop you being permanently on the move on the Atlantic coast is your time

marked tours. Since 2012, it is now possible to cycle the whole way from Brittany to Hendaye on the Spanish border without a break on dedicated paths. The 1200km (750mi)-long route runs the length of the Atlantic coast and forms the longest bike path in France and constitutes the French section of the European cycle network Eurovélo 1. Shorter routes, such as the 112km (70mi)-long *Vélocéan*

between Piriac-sur-Mer and Les Moutiers-en-Retz that passes through a lovely stretch of countryside, are also well maintained and signposted.

You can rent bikes virtually everywhere. *Créon*, 25km (15½mi) to the southeast of Bordeaux in Entre-Deux-Mers, is unique in France having the very first 'bike station'. Like in a ski resort, you can hire everything you need in one place. A map 'À vélo en

Aquitaine' can be downloaded from the website of the Comité Régional de Tourisme d'Aquitaine *(www.tourisme-aquitaine.info)*. Tips and suggested routes for tours in the Vendée can be found under *www.velo-loisirs.fr.* High-visibility vests with reflectors must be worn at night and in bad weather outside built-up areas.

DIVING

The undersea world off the rocky Côte Basque is especially interesting. Diving schools can also be found further to the north along the Atlantic coast, such as in La Baule, Arcachon and Biscarrosse.

FISHING

In the peak season, fishing from the beach or cliffs is not allowed in many resorts. The inland lakes, canals and rivers are ideal for freshwater fishing. Sea fishing trips are available from a number of harbours on the coast. A fishing licence – only needed for inland lakes – costs 4–6 euros a day or 15–25 euros for a whole year. General information about fishing grounds and licences is available from the *Fédération Française des Pêcheurs en Mer (tel. 05 59 31 00 73 | www.ffpm-national.com)*. For maps and further information see: *www. federationpeche.fr*

GOLF

Golf is a traditional sport especially on the Basque coast. The second oldest golf course in France is *Golf de Biarritz Le Phare (www.golf-biarritz.com)*. But there is no shortage of beautiful greens elsewhere, especially in and around Biarritz where there are 10 to choose from. Beginners' courses are available at 5 schools in the *Centre International d'Entraînement au Golf d'Ilbarritz (Avenue du Château | tel.*

05 59 43 81 30 | www.golf-ilbarritz.com) in *Bidart*, where you can practice your shots on the cliffs.

HIKING

When hiking, you can experience the area's greatest attractions – the coast and the marshlands – that much more intensely, especially in the nature reserves on the Côte de Lumière. Such routes include those through the Marais de l'Eguille or the Forêt Domanial on Oléron (waymarked routes) or opposite, on the mainland, INSIDER TIP through the Bourcefranc-le-Chapus oyster farming region.

LAND YACHTING

At low tide the wide beaches down the Atlantic coast provide perfect conditions for land yachting. One hotspot is *Notre-Dame-de-Monts (Centre de Char à Voile | www.charsavoile.com)* with its almost 30km (19mi)-long beach. The 3-wheeled vehicles with sails *(chars à voile)* can be hired at yachting schools.

PARAGLIDING

Favourable winds in summer make taking off from the Dune du Pilat with a paraglider (or similar) easy. The dune is the biggest paragliding zone in the world Prerequisites are nerves of steel and a 10-hour training session (e.g. at *Sand Fly École de Parapente | Arcachon | tel. 06 63 21 27 82 | www.sand-fly.com)*.

RAFTING

Whitewater tours on rubber dinghies are available on rivers in the Pyrenees in the Basque Country in particular. Information from the *Ligue d'Aquitaine de Canoë-Kayak (tel. 05 57 22 29 89)*. Tours on the Nive are offered from Itxassou *Évasion Montagne Eaux Vives (Maison Errola | tel. 05 59 29 31 69 | www.evasion64.fr)*, for example.

RIDING

Whether along the beach, through salt-marshes, vineyards or in the Pyrenees, there are 8500km (5300mi) of way-marked bridleways to choose from. Hacks and excursions lasting several days are available. Information and addresses can be obtained from the *Comité Régional de Tourisme Equestre d'Aquitaine (tel. 06 08 60 56 67 | www.cheval-aquitaine.com)*.

SAILING

Sailing schools and boat rental companies are ten a penny. The tourist information office in each resort has a list of addresses. The French sailing association has given certain seaside resorts a quality seal of approval – the 'Station voile' (e.g. *La Teste-de-Buch, Arcachon* and *Hendaye*). The 'France Station Nautique' label is a guarantee for an extensive range of watersports which always includes sailing.

STAND-UP PADDLING

The latest watersport trend is stand-up paddling. You stand on a particularly long and stable surfboard and propel yourself forward with a paddle. Keeping your balance is easier than it sounds which accounts for this new fun sport's rapidly growing popularity. Available e.g. from *Surf en Pays de Buch (tel. 06 80 05 46 95 | www.sup-arcachon.com)*. Paddling can also be done on rivers inland, on the Dordogne in Périgord, for example *(Sup-Périgord | Le Couderc | Cénac-et-Saint-Julien | www.sup-perigord.com)*.

SURFING & WINDSURFING

The French Atlantic Coast is one of the world's hotspots for surfing, especially Hossegor and Biarritz. A list of clubs that belong to the French surfing association can be found under *www.surfingaquitaine.com*. For general information see: *Fédération Française de Surf (tel. 05 58 43 55 88 | www.surfingfrance.com)*. The inland lakes are ideal for windsurfing. Most sailing schools rent out equipment too.

Beach boys are in their element on the Atlantic coast

TRAVEL WITH KIDS

France caters well for children (and their parents) in everyday life and on holiday – be it child minding or entertainment, and restaurants have highchairs and cheap *menus enfants* for families.

In most seaside resorts the question 'What can I do?' is easily answered: 'Mickey Club!' – supervised games and sports for children aged 3–14.

Particularly family-friendly accommodation, facilities and events have been given the 'Station Kid' award. Things on offer include surfing, sailing and canoeing especially tailored to children's needs. Many places on the Atlantic are near an inland lake that is safer to swim in.

LES MACHINES DE L'ÎLE IN NANTES
(128 C3) (*∅ C4*)

Entertainment for the whole family in the old docklands in Nantes. Mechanical sea and mythical creatures can be ridden on a merry-go-round. A real highlight are the trips on a reeling boat, which involves being sprayed with water (macks are provided). Rides on the 12m (40ft) *Grand Éléphant* are also very popular not just among the young. *Les Chantiers (Boulevard Léon-Bureau, April–June and Sept/Oct Tue–Sun 10am–5pm, July/ Aug daily 10am–8pm, Nov/Dec and*

Photo: Étang d'Aureilhan near Mimizan

Water, sand, lots of amusement parks and a sight-seeing train in the Pyrenees: there are plenty of things for children to do here

mid Feb–March Wed–Sun 2pm–5pm | entrance fee and elephant ride 7 euros each, children (aged 4–18) 5.50 euros | www.lesmachines-nantes.fr

PIRIAC AVENTURE IN PIRIAC
(128 A2) (*M A3*)

Tree canopy adventure for children aged 4+ along various different routes. Also for parents. Hanging from a wire rope or clambering through pipes and across bridges – but always safely harnessed. A similar park is in Pornic *(www.pornic-aventure.com)*. *Route de Mesquer | July/ Aug daily 9am–7.30pm, April–June Wed, Sat, Sun 10am–7pm, Sept/Oct Wed, Sat, Sun 1pm–7pm | 21 euros, children (depending on age) 15, 17 or 19 euros, concessions for families and groups | www.piriac-aventure.com*

PLANÈTE SAUVAGE IN PORT SAINT-PÈRE (128 C3) (*M C4*)

This extensive animal reserve has a 10km (6¼mi) drive-through safari route where you can see animals from 5 continents. Sea lions perform tricks in the Cité Marine and in the village there is a flamingo island, a monkey forest and a reptile house. *La Chevalerie | July/Aug daily 9.30am–8pm, April–June and Sept 10am–7pm, March and Oct 10am–6pm | various rates from 18 euros upwards | www.planetesauvage. com*

CÔTE DE LUMIÈRE

AQUARIUM LA ROCHELLE (130 B2–3) (*M D7*)

Fascinating aquarium with masses of different sea creatures to see – all presented perfectly with young visitors in mind. The fish tanks are at the right height for a child and a trip in the 'lift' puts everyone in the right mood: water shoots up behind the glass walls as if you were really going down to the bottom of the sea. *Bassin des Grands Yachts | July/Aug daily 9am–11pm, April–June and Sept 9am–8pm, Oct–March 10am–8pm | 14.50 euros, children (aged 3–17) 11 euros | www.aquarium-larochelle. com*

CENTRE AQUATIQUE IN CHÂTELAILLON-PLAGE (130 B–C3) (*M D7*)

Water park with slides, several pools and a water temperature of 29°C (84,2°F). *RN137 | July/Aug Mon–Fri 10am–8pm, Sat 11.3pm–8pm, Sun 9am–8pm, times vary other months | 5.20 euros, children (aged 3–16) 3.80 euros | www.centre-aquatique. com*

L'ÎLE AUX PAPILLONS ON NOIRMOUTIER (128 B4) (*M B4*)

Exotic butterflies from Guyana, Kenya, Madagascar and the Philippines in a jungle environment. *5, Rue de la Fassonière | La Guérinière | June–Aug daily 10am–7.30pm, April, May, Sept Mon–Fri 2pm–7pm, Sat/Sun 10.30am–7pm | 7.80 euros, children (aged 3–12) 5.70 euros | www.ile-aux-papillons.com*

INSIDER TIP JARDIN DU VENT IN NOTRE-DAME-DE-MONTS (128 B4) (*M B5*)

(Hands-on) devices in this wonderful open-air display let you see, hear and feel the wind which blows continuously in the Vendée. The wind makes music, blows bubbles and envelops visitors in a scented cloud. *29, Rue Gilbert Cesbron | June–Aug Mon–Fri 10am–7pm, Sat/Sun 2pm–7pm, April, May, Sept Tue–Sun 2pm–6pm | 4 euros, children (aged 6–18) 2.20 euros*

ZOO DE LA PALMYRE (130 B4) (*M D9*)

Aminals from 5 continents, including tigers, leopards, giraffes, kangaroos and polar bears can be seen here in in large enclosures that give the animals as much freedom as possible. *La Palmyre | April–Sept daily 9am–7pm, Oct–March 9am–6pm | 15 euros, children (aged 3–12) 11 euros | www.zoo-palmyre.fr*

CÔTE D'ARGENT

LA FORÊT DE L'AVENTURE IN MONTALIVET (130 B6) (*M D10*)

Play at being Tarzan (while safely hooked on in a harness) in the treetops. There is an 'Explorer Route' (min. height 1.10m/3'7'') and an 'Adventurer Route' (1.40m/4'7''). *Lède de Montalivet | July/Aug daily 10am–8pm, April–June and Sept/Oct Sat 2pm–6pm, Sun 2pm–5.45pm | depending on route 18–20 euros, children taller than 1.40m 17 euros, 1.10m or upto 5 years 13 euros, upto 5 years 7.50 euros | www.laforet-aventure.com*

LA HUME IN THE BASSIN D'ARCACHON (132 A4) (⨭ D12)

Here you can find 4 completely different parks in one: *Aqualand*, *La Coccinelle* zoo with more than 800 animals, a large *botanical garden* and *Kid's Parc*, a scaled-down world for children to explore – also interesting for parents. *La Hume | June—Sept daily 10am–6pm, botanical garden 10am–12.30pm and 2.30pm–7pm | 7–15 euros per park*

PORT MINIATURE IN SOUSTONS (134 C3–4) (⨭ C–D15)

Play at being captain of a Mississippi paddle steamer or explore the seas on the historic sailing ship – the 'Mayflower' – on the Lac de Soustons. Suitable for children aged 9+. The boats can take up to 6 people. *July/Aug daily 10am–7pm | 4.50 euros per person per 15 mins. | www.loisirs-soustons.com*

ZOO DU BASSIN D'ARCACHON IN LA TESTE (132 A4) (⨭ D12)

One of the largest zoos in France covering 24 acres of forest land near Arcachon. Including pets' corner where the animals can be stroked. *Route de Cazaux | La Teste-de-Buch | mid April–mid Sept daily 10am–7pm, Feb–mid April and mid Sept–mid Nov Wed, Sat, Sun 2pm–6.30pm | 15 euros, children (aged 2–12) 10 euros | www.zoodubassindarcachon.com*

CÔTE BASQUE

MUSÉE DE LA MER AQUARIUM IN BIARRITZ (134 B5) (⨭ C16)

A perfect destination for the whole family with several thousand species and modern, interactive displays. Older children will also love the adjoining Cité de la Mer. *Esplanade du Rocher de la Vierge, July/Aug daily 9.30am–midnight, April–June and Sept/Oct 9.30am–8pm, Nov–March*

9.30am–7pm | 13 euros, children (aged 4–16) 9.50 euros, combined ticket with Cité de la Mer 16.50 euros, children 12 euros | www.museedelamer.com

A young technician inspecting a hydrant

FESTIVALS & EVENTS

FESTIVALS & EVENTS

JANUARY

▶ *La Folle Journée de Nantes* – an annual series of classical music concerts in and around Nantes (usually on the last weekend); the biggest event of its kind in the country. *www.follejournee.fr*

WHITSUN

Saint-Gilles-Croix-de-Vie in the Vendée is the setting of the weekend international jazz festival ▶ *Saint Jazz sur Vie.* *www.saint-jazz-sur-vie.com*

JUNE

▶ *Fête du Printemps* in Saint-Émilion with procession (3rd Sun), when the wine-makers declare the quality of the new wine.

Some 1000 marathon runners attend the ▶ *Maraisthon* in the Marais Poitevin nature reserve (3rd Sun) with twice that number of spectators in Coulon. For the less energetic, 2 hiking trails are waymarked (10 or 11km/6¼ or 6¾mi). *www.poitou-charentes-vacances.com*

On even years, Bordeaux stages the ▶ *Bordeaux Fête le Vin* (late June/early July). *www.bordeaux-fete-le-vin.com*

JULY

Young and established artists and orchestras participate in the ▶ INSIDER TIP **Musique au Cœur du Médoc** event in châteaux and monasteries in Médoc – followed by wine tasting. *www.estivales-musique-medoc.com*

▶ *Fête du Thon* (2nd weekend) in Saint-Jean-de-Luz with street music and tuna specialities.

On ▶ *Bastille Day* (14 July), celebrations – usually starting the evening before – are everywhere. Big fireworks displays.

▶ *Biarritz Surf Festival* (3rd week) in Biarritz. The world's best surfers then

Marathons, jazz and classical music, fireworks and fish, archaic displays of strength and wine, wine and more wine

go to the ▶ *Roxy Jam Biarritz* shortly afterwards.

JULY/AUGUST

▶ *Fête de la Sardine* in La Turballe (mid July, repeated mid August).

▶ *Bataille de Castillon* (*www.bataille decastillon.com*) in Castillon-la-Bataille. Annual re-enactment of the battle between England and France that ended the 100 Years' War in 1453 and the British occupation.

The ▶ *Jazz and Wine* festival with big names and famous wines in several *châteaux* in Médoc. *www.jazzandwine.org*

AUGUST

The ▶ *Force Basque* test of strength (mid Aug) in Saint-Palais: tug-of-war, wood chopping and stone-lifting.

140 wooden sailing boats battle it out at the weeked (around the 15th) at the ▶ *Regates du Bois de la Chaise* off Noirmoutier.

Arcachon's ▶ *Fête de la Mer* (mid Aug) with fireworks, lots of music and a huge picnic on the beach.

▶ *Nuit Féerique* (mid Aug) in Biarritz also with a huge firework display.

The jazz and world music festival ▶ *Les Rendezvous de l'Erdre* (*www.rendezvouserdre. com*) in Nantes takes place on 4 days at the end of Aug on the banks of the Erdre.

SEPTEMBER

7000 runners, most in costumes, take part in the ▶ *Médoc-Marathon* on the 2nd weekend (*www.marathondumedoc.com*).

OCTOBER

▶ *Course des Garçons de Café* (end Oct) on uneven years – when waiters in Saint-Émilion balance their trays through the town's narrow streets.

LINKS, BLOGS, APPS & MORE

LINKS

▶ www.flickr.com/photos/tourisme-aquitaine Photos of the French Atlantic Coast to whet your appetite for more

▶ www.rando64.fr All you need to know about hiking inland from the Côte Basque, with tips for riders, cyclists, mountainbikers and even for those who fancy a snowshoe hike in the Pyrenees

▶ www.gites-de-france-gironde.com, www.gites-de-france-landes.com, www.gites-sud-atlantique.com Masses of addresses for those looking for that perfect holiday cottage

▶ www.thalassocotebasque.com Information and addresses of seawater therapy centres on the Basque coast

▶ www.frenchatlantic.worldweb.com Useful information when planning your holiday, including maps, a tourism directory listing accommodation and sights, as well as restaurants, shops, rental companies, etc.

VIDEOS & STREAMS

▶ www.youtube.com/user/MuseeMer64 A collection of videos on the Musée de la Mer in Biarritz

▶ www.youtube.com/watch?v=VI2QUoFTzmo Direct 8 TV programme about the Basque Country from the 'À vos régions' series – in French but with all sorts of impressions of the area

▶ www.viewsurf.com Website with links to countless webcams at surfing hotspots in the whole of France, incl. more than 100 on the French Atlantic Coast

Regardless of whether you are still preparing your trip or already on the French Atlantic Coast: these addresses will provide you with more information, videos and networks to make your holiday even more enjoyable

APPS

▶ The world-class wines of Médoc near Bordeaux General information about the big names in the area, tips for visits to châteaux and what to order when dining

▶ Royan tour A guided tour of Royan with addresses and information on restaurants, accommodation, beaches, events, etc.

▶ Girondins Officiel For football fans who need their daily dose of sport! All you need to know about the team from Bordeaux

BLOGS & FORUMS

▶ www.telegraph.co.uk/travel/destinations/europe/france/8526267/Camping-in-France-Perfect-pitches-on-the-Atlantic-coast.html A personal selection of campsites down the Atlantic coast

▶ www.marysvendee.com/ 'A little taste of paradise' – the Vendée region from sea level to the treetops, from flea markets to wine tasting: a personal tour of this lovely area

▶ www.expat-blog.com/en/directory/europe/france All sorts of weird and wonderful things can happen when living in a foreign country. Just read the blogs of those who have settled in Bordeaux and Nantes!

▶ http://french.about.com/od/blogs/French_Blogs.htm A collection of blogs about France, some in French, about the French language and France in general – including some tips for learning French

NETWORK

▶ http://fr-fr.facebook.com/gitesdefrance.landes.sudouest On Facebook: information about small, personally run places to stay in the southwest of France

▶ twitter.com/#!/so_biarritz Pining for the southwest corner of France? Under @SO_Biarritz you can find out up-to-the-minute information from this beautiful town in the Basque Country – from the weather to events, dates of concerts, etc. and what makes the people of Biarritz tick

TRAVEL TIPS

ARRIVAL

✈ A number of national as well as budget airlines fly from various major and provincial UK airports to Bordeaux and Nantes, as well as Biarritz, Pau and Bergerac. It is worth spending some time looking for the best connections and comparing prices, e.g. under *www.flybe.com, www.easyjet.co.uk, www.britishairways. com* (e.g. Gatwick–Bordeaux) and *www. airfrance.co.uk* (e.g. Heathrow–Pau), or ask your local travel agent.

🚗 Crossing the Channel from England, the best route from Calais to the French Atlantic Coast is via Paris and then on the A11 motorway Paris–Le Mans–Nantes (384 km/240mi) or on the A10 via Tours and Poitiers to La Rochelle or Bordeaux (560 km/350mi). Alternatively, if you cross to Le Havre or Cherbourg, it is best to head for Le Mans or Rennes respectively. If you are going to the Basque Country, the long crossing from Plymouth to Bilbao in Spain may be a viable alternative.

🚆 The high-speed train, TGV, covers the distance Paris–Nantes in 2 hrs., Paris–Bordeaux in 3. The Eurotunnel shuttle service between Folkestone and Calais operates 365 days a year with up to 4 departures an hour *(www.eurotunnel. com/uk/home)*. Those travelling to the Côte d'Argent and Côte Basque can take the TGV to the Spanish border. Advance reservation necessary.

BANKS & CREDIT CARDS

Cashpoint terminals (ATMs) can be found on virtually every corner (for EC and credit cards). Credit cards are widely accepted in hotels, restaurants, shops and garages in France (esp. Visa and Eurocard), even for smaller amounts.

CAMPERVANS

The Atlantic coast boasts masses of campsites and is ideal for holidaying with a campervan. The *Guide Officiel des Étapes Touristiques en Camping Car* lists 1700 addresses of interest in France. Although many campsites have pitches for campervans, sometimes these are not suitable.

CAMPING

Campsites of all categories are two a penny. In the forests and dunes on the Côte d'Argent in particular, one site rubs shoulders with the next. Nevertheless reservations are necessary in the high season. An overview of all campsites (plus

RESPONSIBLE TRAVEL

It doesn't take a lot to be environmentally friendly whilst travelling. Don't just think about your carbon footprint whilst flying to and from your holiday destination but also about how you can protect nature and culture abroad. As a tourist it is especially important to respect nature, look out for local products, cycle instead of driving, save water and much more. If you would like to find out more about eco-tourism please visit: *www.ecotourism.org*

From arrival to weather

Holiday from start to finish: the most important addresses and information for your trip to the French Atlantic Coast

links) can be found on the website of the Fédération Française de Camping: *www.camping-france.com*

CAR HIRE

Major car hire companies can be found at the airports and in larger towns and cities. A driving licence – which you must have held for at least 1 year – has to be presented. It is almost always cheaper hiring a car and organising insurance before travelling, especially in the high season. On arrival always check the car for scratches or dents and make sure the tank has been filled up. Avoid taking out additional insurance – this is generally superfluous and can lead to unnecessary costs.

CONSULATES & EMBASSIES

BRITISH CONSULATE

353, Boulevard du Président Wilson | 33073 Bordeaux | tel. +33 5 57 22 21 10 | ukinfrance.fco.gov.uk/en

CONSULATE OF THE UNITED STATES OF AMERICA

89, Quai des Chartrons | 33300 Bordeaux | tel. +33 5 56 48 63 85 | bordeaux.usconsulate.gov

CUSTOMS

UK citizens do not have to pay any duty on goods brought from another EU country as long as tax was included in the price and the items are for private consumption only. Tax free allowances include: 800 cigarettes, 400 cigarillos, 200 cigars, 1kg pipe tobacco, 10L spirits, 20L liqueurs, 90L wine, 110L beer.

BUDGETING

Coffee	from £2.40/$3.90
	for a café crème
Ice cream	£1.20–1.60/$2–2.60
	for a scoop of ice cream
Wine	from £1.60/$2.60
	for a glass of wine
Sandwich	from £3/$4.80
	for a ham and cheese baguette
Petrol	approx £1.20/$1.90
	for 1L super unleaded
Bicycles	£8–10/$13–16
	rental charge per day

Those travelling from the USA, Canada, Australia or other non-EU countries are allowed to enter with the following tax-free amounts: 200 cigarettes or 100 cigarillos or 50 cigars or 250g pipe tobacco. 2L wine and spirits with less 22 vol. % alcohol, 1L spirits with more than 22 vol. % alcohol content.

American passport holders returning to the USA do not have to pay duty on articles purchased overseas up to the value of $800, but there are limits on the amount of alcoholic beverages and tobacco products. For regulations for international travel for U.S. residents see *www.cbp.gov*.

DRINKING WATER

Tap water is safe to drink *(eau potable)* and in restaurants the locals tend to prefer the *carafe d'eau* to expensive mineral water. In many towns and villages there are public water fountains.

CURRENCY CONVERTER

£	€	€	£
1	1.20	1	0.85
3	3.60	3	2.55
5	6	5	4.25
13	15.60	13	11
40	48	40	34
75	90	75	64
120	144	120	100
250	300	250	210
500	600	500	425

$	€	€	$
1	0.75	1	1.30
3	2.30	3	3.90
5	3.80	5	6.50
13	10	13	17
40	30	40	50
75	55	75	97
120	90	120	155
250	185	250	325
500	370	500	650

For current exchange rates see www.xe.com

DRIVING

With few exceptions, you have to pay to travel on French motorways. Pay at *péage* toll booths in cash or with a credit card. If you break down, emergency phones are 2km (1¼mi) apart. Main roads *(routes nationales)* are generally good but correspondingly heavily used. Speed limits: 130 km/h (80 mph) on motorways (110 km/h/68 mph when raining); 110 km/h (68 mph) on dual carriageways (100 km/h/ 62 mph when raining); 90 km/h (55 mph) on *routes nationales* and *routes départementales* (80 km/h/50 mph when raining); 50 km/h (30 mph) in built-up areas. Motorbikes must have dipped headlights on at all times; this also applies to all other vehicles when raining or foggy. A warning triangle and high-visibility jacket with reflectors must be carried in the car at all times. The legal drink-driving limit is 50mg per 100ml of blood. Since 2012, all drivers must carry a portable breath-testing kit in the car to be able to test themselves that they are within the limit. If you do not have an (unused) device with you, you risk being fined. The kits cost approx. 1 euro at garages and in many supermarkets. Channel ports sell them too for around £2.

EMERGENCY SERVICES

The emergency number is *tel. 112*

HEALTH

If you are a UK resident, before going abroad apply for a free European Health Insurance Card (EHIC) from the NHS which allows you access to medical treatment while travelling. It is worth noting that the new European health card is not (yet) being accepted by doctors in France as French card machines are only set for the local plastic cards. Private medical travel insurance is highly recommended.

IMMIGRATION

A valid passport is required for entry into France. All children must travel with their own passport. Citizens of EU countries, the USA and Canada do not need visas to visit France as tourists for a stay of less than three months.

INFORMATION

ATOUT FRANCE
– *Lincoln House, 300 High Holborn | London WC1V 7JH | tel. 207 061 66 00 | www.atout france.fr; www.rendezvousenfrance.com*

REGIONAL TOURIST INFORMATION OFFICES

- *Pays de la Loire (Côte d'Amour): 1, Place de la Galarne | 44202 Nantes | tel. 02 40 89 89 89 | www.enpaysdelaloire.com*
- *Vendée (Côte de Lumière): 45, Boulevard des États-Unis | 85000 La Roche-sur-Yon | tel. 02 51 47 88 20 | www.vendee-tourisme. com*
- *Charente-Maritime (Côte de Lumière): 85, Boulevard de la République | 17076 La Rochelle | tel. 05 46 31 71 71 | www. en-charente-maritime.com*
- *Gironde (Côte d'Argent, Bordelais): 21, Cours de l'Intendance | 33000 Bordeaux | tel. 05 56 52 61 40 | www. tourisme-gironde.fr*
- *Landes (Côte d'Argent): 4, Avenue Aristide Briand | 40012 Mont-de-Marsan | tel. 05 58 06 89 89 | www.tourisme landes.com*
- *Béarn-Pays Basque (Côte Basque): 4, Allées des Platanes | 64100 Bayonne | tel. 05 59 30 01 30 | www.tourisme64.com*

INFORMATION WEBSITES

Most websites of the tourist information offices in towns and cities as well as regional sites are also in English. These provide practical tips and comprehensive information on what to see and where to stay. Films/videos and live webcams give a good impression of the various holiday destinations. The following websites provide useful general information:
- *www.frenchatlantic.worldweb.com:* practical travel tips with tourism directory, tours, events, accommodation, sights, etc.
- *http://about-france.com/tourism/french-seaside-coast.htm:* information on the coastlines and beaches in France in general with a section on the Atlantic coast
- *www.france-atlantic.com/charente/ la-rochelle-tourist-information.asp:* information on La Rochelle and the Charente-Maritime département

- *www.bordeaux-tourisme.com/index_ uk.html:* comprehensive information website on the World Heritage Site, wine-tasting, practical and cultural information

INTERNET ACCESS & WI-FI

Internet cafés can be found in most resorts and towns and cities. The vast majority of hotels provide free Wi-Fi access.

MOSQUITOES

Mosquitoes can be a nuisance in the evenings especially on lakes and rivers inland but also sometimes on the coast too. Mosquito repellent is a must in your luggage.

NUDISM

Naturisme, as the French call it, is very popular in France. On the Côte d'Argent in particular there are lots of nudist holiday complexes. These *domaines naturistes* are usually well equipped campsites, some with bungalows to rent, with sports and leisure facilities. In other areas, there are virtually always sections of the beach or bay where nude bathing is tolerated. These are however often not manned by lifeguards. Topless bathing is possible on all beaches.

OPENING HOURS

Unless otherwise stated, the opening times given in this guidebook apply to the summer season. In the low season small museums in particular are only open on certain days or by prior appointment.

PERSONAL SAFETY

Normal precautions – like anywhere else in the world – should be taken when holidaying on the French Atlantic Coast. Don't leave valuables in parked vehicles or anything visible that could attract car thieves and be careful of pickpockets (also on the beach).

PHONE & MOBILE PHONE

There are fewer and fewer telephone boxes now in France as well. Most of those that do still exist are card phones. A *télé-carte* can be bought at tobacconists, post offices and garages. The west of France is covered by several mobile phone networks. Ask your provider which French network is the cheapest for your needs and switch over to this manually if another, more expensive partner is selected automati-

cally. Prepaid cards can also be bought at post offices and tobacconists. These often work out cheaper. Text messaging is always cheap. Mailboxes cause high costs – you should switch off this function before going on holiday. The international code for calling France from abroad is *+33*. To call other countries, dial the country code (UK *+44*, US *+1*, Ireland *+353*), and then the telephone number without *0*.

POST

Letters and postcards to EU countries cost 70 cents. Post offices are generally open *9am–noon* and *2pm–5pm, in larger towns 6.30pm, Mon–Fri and 9am–noon Sat. www.laposte.fr.* You can also buy

WEATHER IN BORDEAUX

	Jan	Feb	March	April	May	June	July	Aug	Sept	Oct	Nov	Dec
Daytime temperatures in °C/°F	9/48	11/52	15/59	17/63	20/68	24/75	25/77	26/79	23/73	18/64	13/55	9/48
Nighttime temperatures in °C/°F	2/36	2/36	4/39	6/43	9/48	12/54	14/57	14/57	12/54	8/46	5/41	3/37
Sunshine hours/day	3	4	6	7	8	8	8	8	7	5	3	2
Precipitation days/month	16	13	13	13	14	11	11	12	13	14	15	17
Water temperatures in °C/°F	10/50	10/50	10/50	11/52	13/55	15/59	17/63	17/63	16/61	15/59	13/55	11/52

stamps from tobacconists when you purchase a postcard.

PRICES

Average admission prices to museums, gardens, châteaux and other tourist sights are 2.50–7 euros for adults with children paying around half. Amusement parks are considerably more expensive. There are concessions (50%) for students with a valid international student pass in museums.

PUBLIC TRANSPORT

In Nantes, La Rochelle and Bordeaux, trams, buses, ferries and electric vehicle rental points are very well organised. Environmental awareness is high. City tourist passes that offer reduced or free entrance to attractions include the free use of public transport. In rural areas, however, you generally need a car. To save taking a car on a ferry, bikes can be rented everywhere. Regional trains (TER) operate between urban centres as do coaches run by the French railway company, SNCF. *www.voyages-sncf.co.uk*

TAXI

Taxis are not any one colour in France but must have a 'Taxi' sign on the roof. If it is lit up, the taxi is for hire. Taxi ranks are marked with a blue street sign with 'Taxi' written in white. Different fares apply at night. Check fare prices under: *www.taxis-de-france.com*

TIME

France is one hour ahead of Greenwich Mean Time, six hours ahead of US Eastern Time and eight hours behind Australian Eastern Time.

TIPPING

Add up to 10% to the bill in a restaurant and to a taxi fare. Tips are left in hotels for particularly attentive service. If staying anywhere for a long period, chambermaids are usually given a tip of 10–20 euros a week.

TOURIST TAX

An obligatory *taxe de séjour* is added to the room price in hotels in holiday resorts. Depending on where you are, this is normally 50 cents–1 euro per person, per night.

WHERE TO STAY

The spectrum ranges from youth hostels (information: *FUIAJ | tel. 01 44 89 87 27 | www.fuaj.org)* and *chambres d'hôtes* – the French equivalent to Bed & Breakfast, to luxury hotels. In summer – and especially during the French school holidays – advance booking is absolutely essential. In many hotels on the coast there is a minimum stay of 1 week in the high season; for holiday flats and cottages this is often raised to 2 weeks in July/August.

WEATHER, WHEN TO GO

Everyone in France is out and about from mid July until the beginning of Sept. This is the fullest, hottest and most expensive time of year, and it is absolutely essential to book accommodation in advance. Between June–Sept the Atlantic is warm enough to swim in; the hardy start swimming in May. If you can, travel in the low season. In late autumn, prices drop considerably. This is an ideal time for wine trips, thalossotherapy and city sightseeing.

USEFUL PHRASES FRENCH

IN BRIEF

Yes/No/Maybe	oui/non/peut-être
Please/Thank you	s'il vous plaît/merci
Good morning!/afternoon!/ evening!/night!	Bonjour!/Bonjour!/ Bonsoir!/Bonne nuit!
Hello!/goodbye!/See you!	Salut!/Au revoir!/Salut!
Excuse me, please	Pardon!
My name is ...	Je m'appelle ...
I'm from ...	Je suis de ...
May I ...?/ Pardon?	Puis-je ...?/Comment?
I would like to .../ have you got ...?	Je voudrais .../ Avez-vous?
How much is ...?	Combien coûte ...?
I (don't) like this	Ça (ne) me plaît (pas).
good/bad/broken	bon/mauvais/cassé
too much/much/little	trop/beaucoup/peu
all/nothing	tout/rien
Help!/Attention!	Au secours/attention
police/fire brigade/ ambulance	police/pompiers/ ambulance
Could you please help me?	Est-ce que vous pourriez m'aider?
Do you speak English?	Parlez-vous anglais?
Do you understand?	Est-ce que vous comprenez?
Could you please ...? ... repeat that ... speak more slowly ... write that down	Pourriez vous ... s'il vous plait? répéter parler plus lentement l'écrire

DATE & TIME

Monday/Tuesday	lundi/mardi
Wednesday/Thursday	mercredi/jeudi
Friday/Saturday/ Sunday	vendredi/samedi/ dimanche
working day/holiday	jour ouvrable/jour férié
today/tomorrow/ yesterday	aujourd'hui /demain/ hier
hour/minute	heure/minute
day/night/week	jour/nuit/semaine
month/year	mois/année
What time is it?	Quelle heure est-t-il?

Tu parles français?

"Do you speak French?" This guide will help you to say the basic words and phrases in French

It's three o'clock	Il est trois heures
It's half past three.	Il est trois heures et demi
a quarter to four	quatre heures moins le quart

TRAVEL

open/closed	ouvert/fermé
entrance/exit	entrée/sortie
departure/arrival	départ/arrivée
toilets/restrooms /	toilettes/
ladies/gentlemen	femmes/hommes
(no) drinking water	eau (non) potable
Where is ...?/Where are ...?	Où est ...?/Où sont ...?
left/right	à gauche/à droite
straight ahead/back	tout droit/en arrière
close/far	près/loin
bus/tram/underground / taxi/cab	bus/tramway/métro/taxi
stop/cab stand	arrêt/station de taxi
parking lot/parking garage	parking
street map/map	plan de ville/carte routière
train station/harbour/	gare/port/
airport	aéroport
schedule/ticket	horaire/billet
single/return	aller simple/aller-retour
train/track/platform	train/voie/quai
I would like to rent ...	Je voudrais ... louer.
a car/a bicycle/	une voiture/un vélo/
a boat	un bateau
petrol/gas station	station d'essence
petrol/gas / diesel	essence/diesel
breakdown/repair shop	panne/garage

FOOD & DRINK

The menu, please	La carte, s'il vous plaît.
Could I please have ...?	Puis-je avoir ... s'il vous plaît
bottle/carafe/glass	bouteille/carafe/verre
knife/fork/spoon	couteau/fourchette/cuillère
salt/pepper/sugar	sel/poivre/sucre
vinegar/oil	vinaigre/huile
milk/cream/lemon	lait/crème/citron
cold/too salty/not cooked	froid/trop salé/pas cuit

with/without ice/sparkling	avec/sans glaçons/gaz
vegetarian	végétarien(ne)
May I have the bill, please	Je voudrais payer, s'il vous plaît
bill	addition

SHOPPING

pharmacy/chemist	pharmacie/droguerie
baker/market	boulangerie/marché
shopping centre	centre commercial
department store	grand magasin
100 grammes/1 kilo	cent grammes/un kilo
expensive/cheap/price	cher/bon marché/prix
more/less	plus/moins
organically grown	de l'agriculture biologique

ACCOMMODATION

I have booked a room	J'ai réservé une chambre
Do you have any ... left?	Avez-vous encore ...?
single room/double room	chambre simple/double
breakfast	petit déjeuner
half board/	demi-pension/
full board (American plan)	pension complète
shower/sit-down bath	douche/bain
balcony/terrace	balcon /terrasse
key/room card	clé/carte magnétique
luggage/suitcase/bag	bagages/valise/sac

BANKS, MONEY & CREDIT CARDS

bank/ATM/pin code	banque/guichet automatique/code
cash/credit card	comptant/carte de crédit
bill/coin	billet/monnaie

HEALTH

doctor/dentist/	médecin/dentiste/
paediatrician	pédiatre
hospital/emergency clinic	hôpital/urgences
fever/pain	fièvre/douleurs
diarrhoea/nausea	diarrhée/nausée
sunburn	coup de soleil
inflamed/injured	enflammé/blessé
plaster/bandage	pansement/bandage
ointment/pain reliever	pommade/analgésique

USEFUL PHRASES

POST, TELECOMMUNICATIONS & MEDIA

stamp	timbre
lettre/postcard	lettre/carte postale
I need a landline	J'ai besoin d'une carte téléphonique
phone card	pour fixe.
I'm looking for a prepaid card for	Je cherche une recharge
my mobile	pour mon portable.
Where can I find internet access?	Où puis-je trouver un accès à internet?
dial/connection/engaged	composer/connection/occupé
socket/charger	prise électrique/chargeur
computer/battery/rechargeable	ordinateur/batterie/
battery	accumulateur
at sign (@)	arobase
internet address (URL)/	adresse internet/
e-mail address	mail
internet connection/wifi	accès internet/wi-fi
e-mail/file/print	mail/fichier/imprimer

LEISURE, SPORTS & BEACH

beach	plage
sunshade/lounger	parasol/transat
low tide/high tide/current	marée basse/marée haute/courant
cable car/chair lift	téléphérique/télésiège
(rescue) hut	refuge

NUMBERS

0	zéro	17	dix-sept
1	un, une	18	dix-huite
2	deux	19	dix-neuf
3	trois	20	vingt
4	quatre	30	trente
5	cinq	40	quarante
6	six	50	cinquante
7	sept	60	soixante
8	huit	70	soixante-dix
9	neuf	80	quatre-vingt
10	dix	90	quatre-vingt-dix
11	onze	100	cent
12	douze	200	deux cents
13	treize	1000	mille
14	quatorze		
15	quinze	½	un[e] demi[e]
16	seize	¼	un quart

NOTES

FOR YOUR NEXT HOLIDAY ...

MARCO POLO TRAVEL GUIDES

- PACKED WITH INSIDER TIPS
- BEST WALKS AND TOURS
- FULL-COLOUR PULL-OUT MAP
  AND STREET ATLAS

ROAD ATLAS

The green line ▬▬ indicates the Trips & Tours (p. 96–101)
The blue line ▬▬ indicates The perfect route (p. 30–31)

All tours are also marked on the pull-out map

Photo: Biarritz

Exploring the French Atlantic Coast

The map on the back cover shows how the area has been sub-divided

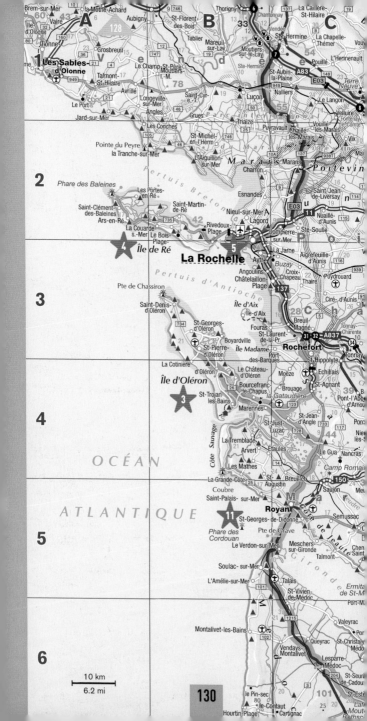

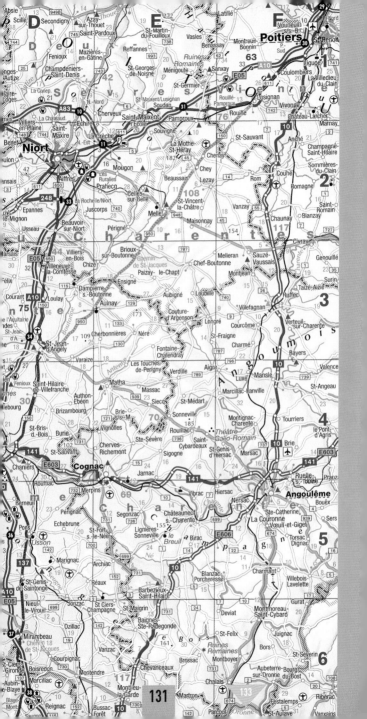

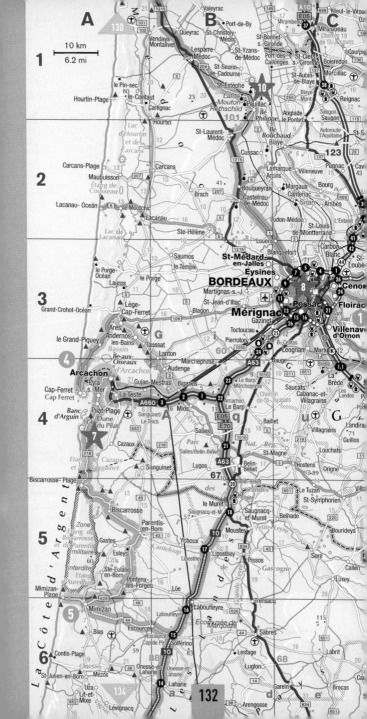

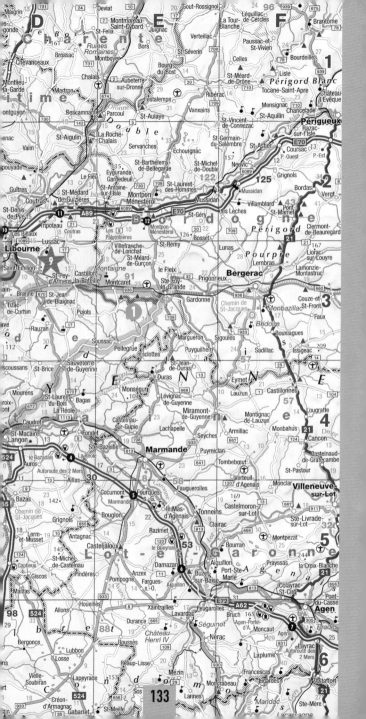

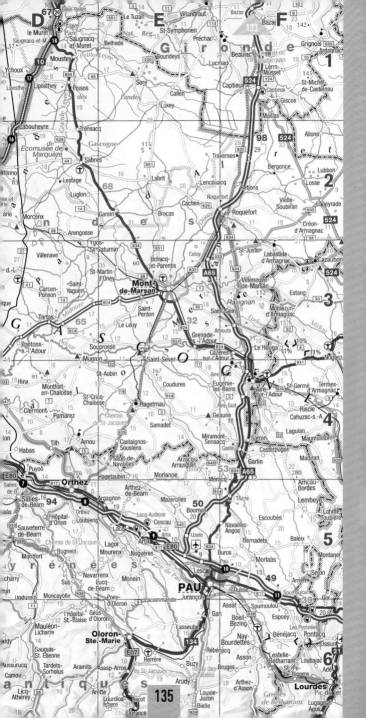

KEY TO ROAD ATLAS

Motorway with junctions	Autobahn mit Anschlussstellen
Motorway under construction	Autobahn in Bau
Toll station	Mautstelle
Roadside restaurant and hotel	Raststätte mit Übernachtung
Roadside restaurant	Raststätte
Filling-station	Tankstelle
Dual carriage-way with motorway characteristics with junction	Autobahnähnliche Schnellstraße mit Anschlussstelle
Trunk road	Fernverkehrsstraße
Thoroughfare	Durchgangsstraße
Important main road	Wichtige Hauptstraße
Main road	Hauptstraße
Secondary road	Nebenstraße
Railway	Eisenbahn
Car-loading terminal	Autozug-Terminal
Mountain railway	Zahnradbahn
Aerial cableway	Kabinenschwebebahn
Railway ferry	Eisenbahnfähre
Car ferry	Autofähre
Shipping route	Schifffahrtslinie
Route with beautiful scenery	Landschaftlich besonders schöne Strecke
Tourist route	Touristenstraße (Alleenstr.)
Closure in winter	Wintersperre (XI-V)
Road closed to motor traffic	Straße für Kfz gesperrt
Important gradients	Bedeutende Steigungen (8%)
Not recommended for caravans	Für Wohnwagen nicht empfehlenswert
Closed for caravans	Für Wohnwagen gesperrt
Important panoramic view	Besonders schöner Ausblick

Of interest: culture - nature (Wartenstein, Umbalfälle)	Sehenswert: Kultur - Natur
Bathing beach	Badestrand
National park, nature park	Nationalpark, Naturpark
Prohibited area	Sperrgebiet
Church	Kirche
Monastery	Kloster
Palace, castle	Schloss, Burg
Mosque	Moschee
Ruins	Ruinen
Lighthouse	Leuchtturm
Tower	Turm
Cave	Höhle
Archaeological excavation	Ausgrabungsstätte
Youth hostel	Jugendherberge
Isolated hotel	Allein stehendes Hotel
Refuge	Berghütte
Camping site	Campingplatz
Airport	Flughafen
Regional airport	Regionalflughafen
Airfield	Flugplatz
National boundary	Staatsgrenze
Administrative boundary	Verwaltungsgrenze
Check-point	Grenzkontrollstelle
Check-point with restrictions	Grenzkontrollstelle mit Beschränkung
Capital (ROMA)	Hauptstadt
Seat of the administration (VENÉZIA)	Verwaltungssitz
Trips & Tours	Ausflüge & Touren
Perfect route	Perfekte Route
MARCO POLO Highlight	MARCO POLO Highlight

INDEX

This index lists all sights and destinations featured in this guide.
Numbers in bold indicate a main entry.